THE TRUTH OF LIFE is discovered within ourselves. But how do we find the way in?

The spiritual teacher is the doorkeeper. Within, the master sits and beckons. In this book we find the authentic voice and teaching of the master – directly addressing us with a challenge, an enticement, to recognise the life or spirit we inwardly know ourselves to be.

Not an account of Barry Long's self-discovery, or anyone's story, this collection of ninety-nine brief essays reminds us that at the core of our being we have no history; we are in essence free and timeless. These are essential statements about truth, love, God, meditation, prayer, the condition of the world and the paths and byways of spiritual and psychic teachings.

'A lucid exploration of the true life lived in spirit. Chapter by chapter, page by page we are taken into the uncharted depths of spiritual being. Any person who reads this book will come to see that Masters do exist among us.' GOLDEN AGE

Also by Barry Long

Meditation: A Foundation Course
Knowing Yourself
Wisdom and Where To Find It
The Origins of Man and the Universe
Stillness Is The Way
Only Fear Dies
Making Love: Sexual Love the Divine Way
To Woman In Love
To Man In Truth
Raising Children in Love, Justice and Truth
Where the Spirit Speaks to Its Own
A Prayer for Life
My Life of Love and Truth

The *Way In*

A book of self-discovery

Plain Statements
of Essential Truth

by

BARRY LONG

BARRY LONG BOOKS

First published in the year 2000
Reprinted 2014

BARRY LONG BOOKS
BCM Box 876 London WC1N 3XX, UK
Box 5277, Gold Coast MC, Queensland 4217, Australia
6230 Wilshire Blvd – Suite 251, Los Angeles, Ca 90048, USA.

Some chapters in this book were originally published
as pamphlets and leaflets by The Barry Long Foundation.
Two parts of the book were written to be recorded as audio books:
The Way of Prayer [originally released on audio cassette as 'The
End of the World'] and The Way of Stillness [originally released on
cassette as 'Start Meditating Now' and still available on compact disc].

Cataloguing-In-Publication Data:
A catalogue record for this book is available from the British Library.
Library of Congress Catalog Card Number: 99-73760.

Paperback: ISBN 978-0-9508050-5-4
Ebook: ISBN 978-1-899324-28-6

Compiled and edited by Clive Tempest

Cover design: Christina Dreesen
Back cover photo: Rita Newman
Other photos: Ambyr & Alan Johnston
except photo p295 Ian Wolstenholme

Digitally printed in UK and USA

THE WAY IN

CONTENTS

CONTENTS

FOREWORD

THIS BOOK IS a journey of self-discovery with a spiritual master. Everyone attracted to it will already have some inkling of what that might mean, and most readers will have been actively engaged in one way or another with the quest for truth or purpose. On the way we have all met the challenges of life and faced the obstacles in our path. But the meeting with the master is a different order of experience. For some the very idea of a spiritual master may itself be the challenge. But what is a master, if not one who has the knowledge and power to overcome every obstacle? Spiritually the master is the consciousness of that power and overcomes all that stands in the way of realising it. Barry Long is a living master; a man who has lived through the obstacles and accepted every challenge, who can say that he has realised life's purpose.

We meet the master in this book as one whose purpose is to open up the way of self-discovery for us, to show us exactly what the world is and what reality is. Whatever point we have reached in the spiritual life, this is an intimate address to the depths of our being. Sometimes it is challenging, as the master must be. Sometimes frightening, as he penetrates the fond images we hold of the world. Sometimes astonishing. Always inspiring.

This is an anthology of Barry Long's writings from the 1980s when he was announcing his teaching to the world. It is a collection of pieces, written for different reasons and gathered from many moments, but the book is really all of a piece, because all the words carry the same energy of direct statement and are directed at the world from the same place, the point from which the consciousness of the master observes the truth and unity of all things.

It is Barry Long's way to publish announcements from time to time, either as free leaflets or advertisements, to declare himself and his teaching to the world. In recent years his spreading reputation has drawn people to him, but when he first began his public teaching, these declarations, articles and advertisements were the means of attracting people to the talks and teachings he was giving, at that time mainly in London and Sydney. The texts, and their tone, would either appeal immediately to the reader or more frequently drive people away. Thus those who responded selected themselves as the people most able to hear the truth he speaks.

The book has been compiled largely from those short articles, announcements and statements, but about a third is based on scripts Barry Long originally wrote to be recorded, including the text of 'Start Meditating Now' a popular audio tape that has been widely distributed since its first release in 1982. Not all of the material in the book has been published before, but everything in it was written between 1979 and 1989; though it has been more recently edited and revised.

The essays and statements each focus closely on a different aspect of truth or reality and taken as a whole form a notebook of spiritual memoranda, in which Barry Long seeks to express ever more finely the essence of what he endeavours to say. More importantly for the reader, the book serves as a course of teaching, a process of self-discovery which becomes ever more revealing the more we read it. The words do not just carry a story and meaning; they are the meaning. They say what they say. The more we pay attention to what's on the page, without assuming anything about what is being said, the more it works for us.

There is an old saying that masters use: 'Contradiction is the way'. In a book that has so many facets, where texts have many strands of meaning, criss-crossing themes repeat themselves and sometimes contradictions may seem to appear. Some things will seem so obvious as not to require saying; some things will startle and others seem blindingly opaque. But later we will read the same thing again, and it will not be the same. In other words, it is the way of this material to speak to us according to our need. It is for you to find your own way of reading it and of using it in your life. It is self-discovery with the master, and in your hands.

Clive Tempest

BEFORE YOU BEGIN

MUCH OF WHAT I am going to say will be new, unsettling and disturbing. It will linger in you. To the extent that you are real it will keep coming up in your awareness. It will cause a lot of self-searching.

Whether you agree or disagree with what is said is unimportant. The only question is: What are you going to do about it? Only you need to know the answer.

The truth has to be told, retold and shown to you in many different ways if it is to penetrate all the places in your mind where the untruth hides, if it is to dissolve your belief in the false, if you are ever going to stop covering up the truth and excusing the unhappiness which is the cause of all problems.

It will take a good while to absorb it all. Each time you come back to the book you will discern new truths, because the spiritual energy released will have been working in your subconscious from before, loosening and breaking up old habitual thought patterns.

If you are serious in the search for what is true – and who is not searching for it in some way or other? – this book and I will bring you closer to the wonder and beauty of life, the life within you, which is life on earth.

Barry Long

THE WAY OF TRUTH

Everything I say is either true or false.
There is no in-between.
But please do not believe me.
Test each statement in your own experience.
Only in that way can you ever know the truth.

The Spirit in You

I help people like you to find the truth of yourself.

WHAT IS THE truth of yourself?

It is freedom and fulfilment: what every man and woman on earth is looking for. Most people are looking for it in the world. And there's nothing wrong with that; provided you realise you can't have freedom or fulfilment in the world until you've found it in yourself. Otherwise you've got to have the aggravation and obstruction in the world that everyone complains of and regards as unavoidable.

Whatever you acquire or achieve, something is still missing. That's why no one in the world, even among the rich and famous, is ever free for long from their troubles and frustrations.

The truth of yourself is the spirit in you. Spirit is a very hazy and difficult word for most people to relate to. And understandably. For what is it? How does the spirit show itself in your everyday life so you can recognise it?

That's the question, isn't it?

To know what's true you've got to know it in your own experience. You have to be extremely practical in the search for the truth and the only way you can know whether a word is real, or just someone else's jargon, is to actually experience what it stands for.

Being a practical and down-to-earth individual, I'm now going to demonstrate the effect of spirit in your own experience; so that you'll always be able to identify it for yourself and not have to depend on the vague notions and confusing beliefs of others.

You know how sometimes you long or yearn for love, truth or peace? How sometimes you long to be free, not really knowing what it is you want to be free of – and especially when you don't have a problem at the time?

You know what it's like to feel love you're just not able to express? Or a deep creative urge you can't express? That kind of longing – you know it, don't you?

That's the spirit in you. It makes you long and yearn for something you just can't give a concrete name to – because what you're longing for, what you've always longed for in this way, is not in the world. It's in you.

You are longing to be re-united with the spirit or truth of yourself within. I say re-united because you weren't always separated from it. That extraordinary spirit is truth, love, freedom and fulfilment – in one complete and astounding package. Once you find it and merge with it, all your doubts, fears, longing and incompleteness vanish – for all time. And, miraculously, so do all your worldly problems.

That is the truth. That is the truth of yourself. That is the focus of my teaching. You'll notice that it is not based on any formal religion, dogma or belief: it is simply self-knowledge.

People do not realise that the nameless longing is a mighty power in them that can be used consciously to bring about this union and self-realisation.

At times the longing will make you sigh and feel unfillably empty. But the longing is not the cruel afflicting thing your mind will try to make it out to be. It is the pure energy of the divine magnet, your divine nucleus, drawing your reluctant, outwardly fixated awareness in towards itself.

You are either ready to use the power or you are not. People who are not ready won't or cannot feel the nameless longing. It is too fine and uncomfortable for them. Their minds quickly translate it into the desire for some object, person or condition in the world. So they chase or worry after it in that form, turning their back on their own power. It never works. There's always something missing; always more aggravation. And in the end of course, they die. But when you stick with the power and use it consciously to unite with the truth of yourself, you discover that there is no death; that you – life – are immortal.

Isn't that what everyone would like to know? Well, it's true. But, again, you have to know it in your own experience; or else it's just another belief, someone else's jargon.

If what I'm saying is meaningful to you, you have the longing in you. You are moved by the spirit, the power, to hear the truth of it. And you have the opportunity now to recognise what's happening in you.

What you do about it is up to you.

The process of self-union is not easy. I know, because it was done in me. Whatever you go through, emotionally or mentally, I've been through. That's why I am able to help others. But I am not a therapist. I work consciously in the spirit, with the spirit. Therapists work in the emotions and the mind. They help get rid of personality problems, but not the one and only problem – which is deeper than the personality. Only the spirit has the power to do that.

The truth – all truth – is in you now, at this moment. But it's buried under all the years of emotional experience you've gathered, particularly your heartbreaks, disappointments, fears, and self-doubts.

You weren't born with these emotions. You acquired them. You were born free – and are free. That is the truth of yourself. But at birth you didn't have the mind to realise this. So you developed a mind. That's what you've been doing all these years. Now you have the mind, with its wonderful ability to realise the truth, but clinging to it and obscuring its natural clarity are all those burdensome and distracting emotions – which you mistake for yourself. I help you to get rid of that rubbish.

You live to find the truth. That's the purpose of living. Living is practical. So the truth must be practical.

People are practical in their jobs, or they wouldn't be able to do them. They're practical in the home, or the place would be in an awful mess. But they are not practical in the truth. So they do not find the truth, know the truth or live it.

How do I know that? —because the truth, being practical, solves the problems of yourself, all your unhappiness; and how many people do you know who are free of problems and unhappiness every moment of their lives? That's how many know the truth.

What I've just said is being practical, isn't it? —getting right down to the nitty-gritty of what you're looking for and what life's about.

The truth works. The way of truth I teach is practical. You have to live it right from the start. That's why it works.

A DECLARATION

I know the truth.

THERE IS NO right question you can ask me about life, death or yourself that I cannot answer. But you must not believe me when I say this. I might be a liar or a fool.

It is my responsibility to demonstrate the truth in your experience. Yours is to endeavour to be still enough to listen.

Have you wondered what living is all about? Why you are here? Where you are going?

Perhaps you have received some answers. But answers are not enough, are they? Answers generate more questions, more doubt. What you are after is the solution, the truth – the end of all questions, all doubt.

I know the truth and I publicly declare that I know it.

Why is such a simple statement so unusual? Because the human race is not engaged in the search for truth. It prefers to live a lie.

Men in the West are not supposed to say such things. And if they do, it tends to cause a defensive reaction of reservation and resentment in the hearer, largely because of shame that someone else (and not yourself) has dared to go against common ignorance and been bold enough to declare the fruits of it.

Many men and women endeavour to create the impression that they know the truth. But because they do not know, they are very careful not to declare and expose themselves.

There are also persons who do not know the truth but who present it to you by quoting authorities outside themselves, usually masters who are safely dead. This tragically perpetuates the fiction that the individual man or woman – you – cannot know the truth in your own right. I know the truth. I do not need to quote others. Therefore all men can know the truth with the same certainty and directness.

As yet, few men and women in this world know the truth. Few are strong enough to kick the herd instinct and go to the end. On the very few occasions I meet one of these people we have nothing really to say, for there is nothing between us, no questions, no doubt – only the certainty of love or life found.

The truth I and they reveal is already inside every man and woman, there to be rediscovered beneath the falsehood everyone erects around themselves. From childhood, with the help of parents, tutors and friends, everyone gradually conceals themselves under this false hood. Groping for life through it, they wonder why they cannot find enduring purpose or love. And always this artificial barrier, this thick habit, is between them, the earth and their fellow man – even the people they love.

Are you ready to be made simple, to start peeling off your false hood? If so, I can relieve you of the pain of your discontent. I can take your self-doubt and your fundamental unhappiness. But the question is: Are you honest enough, straight enough, to part with your pain – to surrender it? Or are you too attached to it to give it up?

The westernised consciousness, with its emphasis on the intellect, is wrapping up the world, East into West. That would not be a bad thing if the intellect were grounded – grounded in the truth of life. But it isn't. The truth of life is death; and the intellect knows nothing about death. The intellect at present is founded in ignorance – man's ignorance in running from the fact that he is going to die.

In spite of man's great intellectual power of invention and discovery, the one phenomenon he refuses to look into is his own death. In the supposed search for it he investigates other people's minds and emotions, other people's bodies and experiences, other people's deaths, but never does he look into himself for the truth, before he dies.

In its flight from the fact and truth of death, the intellect the world over is running wild, out of control. Everyone is being dragged along with it, willy-nilly. Whatever man likes to call it – progress, economic necessity, war for the sake of peace, revolution, business, detente, social advancement – every distinction is irrelevant in the mindless stampede.

My task is to penetrate your intellect and help you to ground it in the truth, which is in yourself and not in your head. You will have to do some dying for this to happen. But when you are through you will no longer be a runner. You will be a centred individual. You will know the truth, the secret of death, the secret of yourself, and you will be free.

I am willing to demonstrate publicly an intelligence superior to that of any man or woman, however highly regarded by the world, whose mind is not grounded in the truth. It is not that I as a person am more intelligent. It is that my involvement with life, my enquiry of life through self-knowledge and the truth of death – the ultimate experience of living – is demonstrably more intelligent than that of any man or woman involved in something else. Hence my knowledge is more significant.

A man is truly only as intelligent as his enquiry of life. The westernised intellect, no matter how gifted, clever or knowledgeable, cannot stand against the truth or consciousness of someone who has realised the truth within. I demonstrate this at every opportunity so that you, my fellow man and woman, can see for yourself that the most brilliant intellect ungrounded in the truth is fundamentally not intelligent.

The final test of intelligence is not the ability to devise, analyse, invent, create, heal or prolong living; but is in being able to understand the mystery of death while still alive, and so help others to understand and participate in that knowledge. This is the beginning of life.

WHAT GOD IS

As I know the truth, I know God.

DOES GOD EXIST?

This question comes straight out of the unintelligent westernised intellect. It has been debated and discussed endlessly in private and public, particularly by the media, without anyone ever getting any closer to the answer. That's because it's a silly question. I'll show you why.

Does 'x' exist?

You can't answer, can you? Before you can answer you have to know what 'x' stands for. You have to define it in your own experience. Before you can say whether gold exists, or anything exists, you've got to know what the word stands for. Then you can look for it and see.

When faced with the opportunity of discovering the truth, the westernised intellect or mind will never ask the right question. So let's ask the right and intelligent question.

What is God?

To the mind this question will seem as debatable as the other. But that is more evasion. To find out, all you have to do is ask someone who knows what God is – just as you would ask someone who knows what gold is – and immediately it will be clear whether the answer is the truth, because the truth is always true in your experience now: you are able to see for yourself.

The trouble is, of course, that the mind thinks it knows what is meant by the word God, when it does not know; or invariably it asks someone who doesn't know what God is, gets the wrong answer and so asks the next wrong question, and the next, and so on. The result is a debate.

I know what God is because I know the truth. So there can be no debate because the answer in truth is always self-evident. So let's see.

God is life.

Look around you. (Take your time to see this.) The room, sky, buildings, traffic, people – the whole acting and inter-acting thing is life: the rush, the standstill, the pain, the slaughter, the joy, the dying, the laughter, the sweetness, the violence, the confusion, the love. Life is everything.

And, most important, see that life or God is not one thing. Nor several things. Life or God is everything – everything at once. Take away one thing, or a million things, and life still goes on. Remove everything-at-once, the whole thing, and the result is what is called death.

So life in its entirety is God. Where there is no life, there is no God. And where there is no God, there is no life. As life is everywhere and is everything now, so is God.

Does God or life exist? Now the question makes sense. And the answer, of course, is instantly obvious.

Forms of life or God exist everywhere: birds, trees, people – even the clouds and buildings can be said to be forms of life, forms of existence. Every thing is a form or condition of life or God.

So God does indeed exist.

Now let's ask another important question.

Is life or God intelligent?

Since it is a right question, the answer is again immediately obvious.

Life or God sustains and recreates its existence perfectly with supreme intelligence, renewing the cells of your body and every body continuously without fuss, doubt or question. Doubters and questioners come and go but life or God goes on, serenely unaffected. The heart beats, the rain falls and the blood and sap flow without the necessity of one human thought; just as the precise moment of birth or of death is determined irrespective of the most earnest human effort or desire, and with the superb detachment of an intelligence that knows exactly what it is doing without any need to be understood. For all things, including querulous man, must obey the same sublime unwavering intelligence, expressing itself as natural laws which the human mind can only minutely reflect or comprehend.

Life or God is intelligence. Even the doubting or agnostic mind is a part of it – its affirmation.

So everything altogether is the existence of the one intelligent life or God in form.

Now we can ask the final question; the one that leads to the ultimate answer.

Where is life itself? Where can life be known direct, without form or beyond form, without doubt, debate or question?

In you. In your body, in your form.

You are the life in your body, aren't you? You know you are alive, don't you? You are the intelligence that knows it, aren't you?

You call it 'I'.

Does God exist?

Is God intelligent?

What is God?

What am I?

You are the living answer.

This is the fundamental discovery of self-knowledge.

HEAR THE TRUTH

Living is not life.

THERE ARE NOT many in the world who can hear the truth, and few of those are moved to do something about it.

If everyone heard the truth the world would run down and stop; and that is not going to happen. In fact, the more men hear the truth, the more frantic is the world's defensive reaction – in its output of useless information and its devotion to the phony notion of progress.

Progress towards what? Do you ever stop to ask?

You start to hear the truth when discontent with the world sets in. That is, when you start running out of tomorrows.

The world's great hold over you is the promise of tomorrow. While you have that, you feel happy and secure. But when your loved one goes, when the money goes, the health goes, the prized possession goes – as each inevitably will – tomorrow vanishes and today becomes a futureless, featureless misery.

Then, in your wretchedness, in your discovery of the world's false promise, you can sometimes hear the truth today.

From the moment you enter the world you are already dying. That is the fact and the truth.

You are the dying living. The world consists of shades and shadows, flitting and fleeting amid the illusion of progress and tomorrow.

The world tells you that you have time. But you have no time. You are going nowhere. The end is the grave.

You can shrug it off for a while but that's where you're going. This is the truth that you and the world are running from. Stop. Stop running. Listen.

You do not need to run. You are running from living – not from life. You have got the two mixed up. Living is not life. Life is what you are, your vital essence. No one can take it from you, ever. But you distance yourself from it – by running.

This life you are is also in the birds, the trees, the sky, the earth. The life you are is the beauty you perceive in these things. It is not in the world, not in tomorrow. It is now.

THE VITAL TRUTH

What is truth?

TRUTH IS THE unshakeable knowledge of your own immortality. It is the realisation of your own true nature, the most profound perception of life.

You are immortal but have not realised it. You sometimes feel it, but that is not enough; the feeling disappears.

Immortality is not the same as survival after death. Survival after death is another tomorrow (hoped for by the surviving few), another escape from the ultimate truth. Because it is a fact that there is no death, all who die physically escape and survive – but then it's too late to know it and live the wonder of it on earth.

There is no abstract or ideal truth. Truth cannot be mentalised. The truth of philosophers is not the truth. If it were, the whole world would be well and truly free by now.

Truth is a living, vital thing. And the nearest living, vital thing you can know and feel at any moment is you.

You are the living truth. You are the truth – living in your body as truly and honestly as you can. The fact that you sometimes feel a failure or see that you have failed, is beside the point. You are doing the best you can. Nevertheless, the truth in you is not complete yet. That is one reason why you are reading this. You want to grow in truth, to grow in knowledge of yourself, into your true nature.

As you have never known an end to yourself, there is no end to truth. But there is a beginning. And this is the point. That beginning is not when you are born. Being born is not the beginning of life. Being born is merely the beginning of living.

'I'm just living. This is not life.' How often have you said that, or felt it?

By living you have to bring yourself to life. That is the purpose of living. And the beginning of truth or life – the much quoted 'moment of truth' – is when you realise with unshakeable knowledge, for all time, that you are immortal life. Only then do you begin.

Before that moment you and everyone living are caught up in the herdal fear of death, obsessed by the need to survive – physically, in fearing the death of the body; emotionally, in fearing the loss of people and things you love or are attached to; and mentally, in the fear of loss and the continual need to defend and reaffirm your beliefs and opinions, even to yourself. The unhappy, competing, warring world and all its institutions are built on this fear of death. With the realisation that you are forever, all the fears and props go.

That is the truth. See it for yourself now, and you are free.

THE PRACTICAL TRUTH

The characteristic of the living truth is practicality.

I AM HERE to teach you the 'new science' of life on earth – how to be unshakeable and authentic without interruption. Until you regain this reality, until you are immersed in it, you will fall back into the old 'present science' caper of abstracting yourself from the truth. You will confuse truth with progress. You will soar up mentally, notionally, out of your body, away from the rich, fulfilling solidity of being what I am here and now, into an airy-fairy, unreal, problem-making and problem-solving world of speculative thought about what you're going to do in the future, what you think you're doing now and what you believe you've done in the past.

You and your Einsteinian society have abstracted you from the vital reality of life. In the necessary activities you are practical. You have to be practical driving your car, or you won't have it for long. You are practical doing your work, or you'll be sacked. But when it comes to what is vital – vitally important things such as your love or sex life, relationships, death, God, discontent, delight, truth and being free – you escape into abstraction. You kid yourself like the scientists that if you concentrate on what is necessary – paying the rent, feeding your children, contributing to progress – you are really living. But what about the inner pain, the doubt, the fear, the hardness, the loneliness, the ache for love?

In abstracting yourself like this from what is vital you make a theory of yourself; and so you spend your days like the theoretical scientist trying to prove yourself, or improve yourself or society – neither of which is real or vital. What is necessary is not vital. The theorising scientists of present science do not know this. Knowing the difference was your problem too, wasn't it? Which is why you need to rediscover the truth of yourself.

All unhappiness is due to not being practical in fact and truth. Losing touch with the truth of yourself as a practical reality naturally makes you self-doubting, insecure, lonely or frustrated. So I keep you earthed in the solid fact of yourself and I give you a practical grounding in truth – no abracadabra, no 'trust me', no 'I believe', no promises; just the simple, precious, self-evident, down-to-earth truth.

The rarest knowledge on this planet is that the truth is practical. The practical truth is for living. Because the teachers and teachings are not practical, the living truth is seldom realised.

The living truth is simply you living it. You are the truth. There is none other. You may be doing your best to live it, but you are not living it uninterruptedly. If you were you would know yourself and be complete every moment without wavering, without collapsing emotionally or in worry under the pressures and circumstances of living. Therefore I will keep you true, true to yourself, true to life.

THE RING OF TRUTH

The truth is in your experience.

How can you know that what I'm saying is the truth?

You know because in the truth there is no authority to refer to outside your own experience.

Let me show you. When you say, 'I love you', only you know whether it is the truth or not. Only you know. No one else on earth knows if you are lying. The truth is in your experience alone.

Perceiving the truth of what I am saying – the truth of yourself as a human being – is as simple as that.

If what I am saying sometimes seems outside your immediate experience you will notice you are unconsciously applying another test. You are listening for the ring of truth.

All the knowledge I express – and it is my only authority – comes spontaneously from my unconscious. At that deep level of human experience it is the same unconscious in you – as in every other man and woman on earth. The ring of truth is the echo of what I am saying, resounding from the truth that is already in you.

You will often find yourself inwardly nodding in agreement, as though I am repeating exactly what you know to be true but have not got round to putting into words.

You will not have read this far if I am talking imaginative nonsense. You are hearing the ring of truth in yourself, the confirming echo sounding off the rock-bed of your unconscious, where all truth lies – even though much of it is as yet unrealised.

GOD'S MIND

Science searches in vain for the missing link.

YOU HAVE PROBABLY heard the quotation from the New
Testament that 'we live and move and have our being in God'.
The westernised intellect has taken the meaning out of the
statement, but I am going to demonstrate the reality of it in your
experience; that is, in practical, down-to-earth self-knowledge.

When I, the individual man or woman, know myself, first I
realise that I am everlasting life. Then I realise that it is God,
I, the formless and inconceivable intelligence in this form,
that contains life.

This is not so surprising, when you look at it, since I am
life or alive in this body or form. In short, I am the intelligent
means by which I know and feel life. I am certainly never
separate from life.

Where life is, I am. Where I am, life is.

Take away this body, as happens when I'm dreaming, and
the 'I' that I then am is indeed just as real as now, although its
form is very much less substantial and consistent.

Remove the dream forms, as happens in dreamless sleep,
and I am as nothing that can be conceived of, named or
remembered. Yet I still am – because I still am next morning
when I wake up in this form. If, while asleep, I had ceased to
be, I would not be able to wake up and remark how well I had
slept. I would not know I had slept well, since there would be
nothing, no 'I', to remember it. But because I was there, and

21

nothing else was, I do not need to remember; I know!

I, the intelligence who knows, am always present in the three modes of existence – in waking, dreaming and dreamless sleep. In each mode of existence the forms change and become less substantial; but I, the essence or intelligence who knows, remain the same throughout.

So what am I?

I am formless, insubstantial, vaster than every form that appears in my perception – and intelligent.

What am I, so that I can perceive the truth of it for myself now, this moment?

The nearest equivalent to formlessness, intangibility and unlimited vastness, is space.

But can space ever be described or demonstrated as being intelligent?

Yes, because space is mind. Your mind is intelligence: every thought and idea you have appears in the space of your mind. You know what you know because you perceive ideas or data from this inner space of mind.

But that's only half of it; the inner half. What about the space you see around your body and every body outside? That is mind too. And every object in it, including yourself, is an idea in that mind. All existence appears in space or mind – in nothing.

The inner space, in which I feel or know that I am alive, or where I sleep, and the outer space, containing all visible existence, together form the totality of God's mind, the divine mind. The real-isation of God's mind – the union of the apparently divided inner and outer space into one perceptive harmony of being – is the consciousness of man who knows himself.

To the scientific and rational westernised intellect, the fact that life itself or God is everything, and contains everything, makes God or life immeasurable; and therefore indiscernible. If you live in space, are space and there is nothing else but space, you cannot measure space. And you are at rest, at peace with yourself. If you start wanting something to do, or to measure, the tension this creates in your inner space (your mind) will manifest as potentially problematical conditions in the space outside you. You will be compulsively attracted to these problems and feel obliged to keep yourself occupied and amused by measuring or attending to them – the very problems or disturbances that you yourself are creating from within!

Scientific and rational knowledge is gained solely from focusing on the observable or measurable universe of space outside yourself – half the mind, the half-truth. It is concerned only with forms or conditions of life that can be weighed, measured or considered. It has no interest in life itself – in the truth of life or divine harmony behind the mind or form, where there are no problems.

Wading through problems in the half-truth of space outside itself, the mind searches in vain for the missing truth, the whole truth that would solve the problem of all problems – the originating disturbance inside the scientist or searcher. Failing to find the truth or solution outside, the human mind settles for various answers – not realising that every answer begets new problems, because every problem in the world is a direct result of the answer to a previous problem. All this creates more tension in the mind, which causes more problems; which creates even more tension. The result? A world or head full of problems. Then what am I? —the problem.

As God's form of existence is existence itself, so the human mind's form of existence is conflict and problems. However, this mind-form is entirely obsessional, created by the mind's tension and ignorance. When the mind sees that there is no problem outside itself, it relinquishes its problematical form. Eventually it realises its own formless harmony and becomes one with the divine mind.

I AM GURU

Who are you?

I AM BARRY LONG, the person in my photograph. But let me declare myself, for the person we say and think we are does not reveal who or what we are; and I do not want to mislead you. I am Guru, the power behind the person and spiritual teacher Barry Long.

There is only one Guru. And I am that. Barry Long is one aspect of my teaching, one of my manifold lives. Since time began I have appeared consciously in the world, declaring myself through enlightened individuals.

Enlightened individuals are those rare men, and even more rarely seen women, who have voluntarily given up their person for my entry into their being as the truth of themselves. I am the truth. To be enlightened is to personify the truth of my presence, to be the living truth. That is the ultimate responsibility of man and woman as life on earth.

Through Barry Long I demonstrate that living truth to people who are ready to hear me. I change them. I awaken them. I bring them back to life. I give them a new place, new space within themselves for a fresh, vibrant beginning. In my presence, in those ready to be themselves, the deadening weight and repetition of the old, the past, begins to crumble.

If you are ready for this fundamental change you are profoundly wearied and discontented with living the limited life of the person you are. You are yearning, searching for something you cannot name, without knowing quite where to look. You long to be true, to be true to life, to be free of fear, expectation and intimidation – the emotional blackmail of your own person and of other people. You long for life and all you can find is living.

You cannot mature and live with your person. There is not enough room in you for both of you. You either start to give the person up now by starting to find or face the truth, the power and the love behind it; or you are stuck with it for another round of time and will have to keep running from the truth of yourself – as you are doing now.

If you think you are happy with the person you are now, I wonder if you will still be as happy when you are told you are dying, when you lose the one you love most or the thing you love most, as you most certainly will; or when it dawns on you once again that you have no purpose in your life and are going nowhere.

The word 'guru' is from Sanskrit, the oldest and truest written language reflecting the truth of life on earth as it once was. When Sanskrit was an active language, Guru, the truth, lived and spoke through many, many, individuals, mostly the elders of the race. To grow old then was not to be geriatric, tolerated, unneeded, useless or helpless, the burden of youth. It was to mature into the dignity of being the living truth, the revered guide, the awakener, the beloved paternal or maternal custodian of the deathless wisdom. Age as experience brought the wisdom of life that is already beyond death; not, as it does today, just the wisdom of living which waits for death.

Westernised society has no word for 'guru', nor concept of it, as it has no time for Guru. Only when time runs out for the individual, when he or she is crushed by the weight of loss, age, sickness or looming death does the person cry out for the truth, love and life – the guidance of Guru.

Where is Guru on the earth today? Are you Guru? Are your parents Guru? Are your friends, teachers or leaders Guru? The distance you and your society are from Guru is the distance you have travelled from the truth of yourself. For Guru – I – am the living truth in you beneath the confusion and anxieties of your troublesome person, which you mistakenly call 'I'.

As Barry Long I speak to the westernised mind not through the inevitable mystique of some darker-skinned guru from the East, but as a man of the West itself. Barry Long was born and has lived his life in this westernised society. My enlightenment of him allows me to perform the extraordinary work of publicly declaring myself to the westernised world as I am doing now. There is no room for misunderstanding or debate in what I am saying. You either hear the truth of it in yourself or you don't. Whether you believe it or not is irrelevant.

In all this I do not want you to get the impression that I am separate from Barry Long. I am Barry Long. There is no duality here, no person to come between and make a problem, a doubt.

As the man I am fully responsible for what I say. I am quite able to confront the most intelligent minds and make sense of what I teach without having to resort to appeals to belief, doctrine or the experience or genius of others. I am new every moment. Nor do I have to conceal my identity behind 'my guru', 'my master', 'my guide', 'my inner voice', or any authority other than myself.

I know myself, therefore I am myself. Being myself I am extraordinarily simple. I am able to speak directly and simply to ordinary people who yearn for love and truth; or who yearn for something greater or more meaningful in their lives than the never-ending complication and self-evasion of what the news and information media consider to be important.

WHO IS BARRY LONG?

See the man and you miss the truth.

BARRY LONG, THE MAN, is finished, dead. Barry Long is a spiritual teaching here solely to help you, the individual, to find the truth of yourself.

Do not be curious about Barry Long the man. Like every man or woman, he is simply the truth he speaks, or the truth he is. Nothing else of him is real. Which is why his body will die; but the truth he is, and speaks, is forever. That is the truth of every human being who is the truth of himself or herself.

Nevertheless, you and I are communicating through the restless, superficial westernised mind. And unless I give the mind some superficial answers to chew on, sooner or later it will get disturbed or peevish about what you have been reading; it will start analysing and speculating and prevent you (who are the intelligent reality behind it) from perceiving the truth.

In what follows I'm going to give a brief personal history. But know that it has no real value unless reading it helps you to see more clearly into the truth of yourself – now. For truth is not in the past. Truth is now.

As you are an ordinary man or woman, I am an ordinary man. I am a product of westernised society. I have married, been a father, raised children, gone to work and found the truth of myself in the West, except for a short stay in India.

I was born in Sydney, Australia, in 1926. As a young man I had a professional career in journalism and public relations. At the age of 31 the involuntary journey inward was begun in me – the descent into my own subconscious, my own ignorance, which is the spiritual path. Eventually, I left my home and family and all that I had accumulated. For fifteen months I lived in India. I found no guru there, nor looked for one. Seeking a guru is unnecessary. Guru is always present on the spiritual path in some form or person – usually in what is afflicting you most. And when you are ready, Guru comes to you consciously in person.

At the age of 38, at Almora in the Himalayas, I passed through a level of the subconscious, its emotional root, where attachment to the fear of death is. I realised immortality, everlasting life as myself, or God immanent.

Four years later, in London, Guru came to me through the person of a younger man who had been my student. For just six weeks this blessed presence stayed and taught or freed me, before returning to cosmic space, or the divine unconscious, leaving behind the purified body and mind of a man who never again would be a student or need a teacher.

Due to the spiritual power of that blessed presence, I penetrated to the deepest level of self-perception where, among other things, detachment from the notion of the physical body occurs. I realised God transcendental, which is the Purusha or divine being of ancient Indian tradition.

In 1977, in preparation for my public entrance into the westernised consciousness, I began teaching meditation and self-discovery to a small circle of men and women at my home in Highgate, London. A year later, I realised the seventh and last level of the terrestrial mind, the place or seat of the Earth Spirit. Here the subconscious and unconscious merge in an energetic, formless unity – paradise or the original garden of all gardens. This is the centre-point of the human psyche out of which arises the divine idea and actuality of life in the garden of planet earth. Here is the indivisible essence of man, all the species and the elements – the perfection and beauty of life on earth that can never be expressed in sense or form, despite the tireless genius of nature. This place, this immortal Eden, as I realised and continue to realise, is man's – all men and women's, beyond the distinction of men and women as different individuals and separate genders. This place itself is the living One, the living beauty, the living sweetness and the living splendour within all life on earth, that has no other life but now and is no other life but now.

In this realisation I am made aware of profound privilege: that I am surrogate for my fellow men and women; and that my function is to report back to them the significance of what I perceive so that they might be helped towards the same reality in themselves. As every realisation imparts an enduring awareness, I continue to be aware of this: it is what I shall be doing, or being, for the rest of my life.

THE QUESTION

Answers are not the solution.

'BUT WHO IS Barry Long? Tell me more . . .'

From answers to questions like this the curious westernised mind has built a global civilisation and culture. Yet not one of the ills of human unhappiness has been cured. Humanity is as tormented as ever by heartbreak, worry, loneliness, anger, death, uncertainty, fear, discontent, frustration and war. In spite of all the questions and unquestionably brilliant answers, every person, sooner or later, ends up back in square one – unhappy.

The reason is that answers do not solve the problem. They merely remove the immediate disquiet or difficulty, before raising more questions about the same problem. Answers in fact prolong the problem; which manifests as the western phenomena of progress and convenience.

There is obviously only one problem. That is human unhappiness. Similarly, there is only one solution. And that is the truth.

To find the solution to unhappiness at any moment – and not avoid or prolong it with phenomenal answers – you simply have to ask the right question. Since the westernised mind never asks the right question, the world never gets rid of unhappiness; and nor do you.

The right question is the question that no one can answer except the questioner.

As this is the truth – the solution to unhappiness at any time – the westernised mind will screw up and pretend it does not understand such a statement.

But you can understand it. You are the truth, the solution behind the problem or unhappiness of the mind itself. All you have to do is keep the mind still and continue to listen.

'Who is Barry Long?' is not a right question.

The right question is: 'Is what he's saying the truth?'

Only you can provide the answer.

If your answer is right it will solve the problem and you will know peace of mind. For the only disturbance in you at any time is the mind's incessant searching for answers.

SELF-REALISATION

I am cosmically conscious.

WHEN I SAY I have 'realised' any truth that I describe, it means I have entered the reality of it as a never-ending participation: the knowledge continues as the living presence of myself.

In the visible world the realisation of anything is the doing of it; otherwise you have only theoretical knowledge which you can learn from a book, remember and forget – unreal knowledge. Do something like drink a cup of tea and without doubt you know the answer to every question about what the experience of drinking a cup of tea is. The knowledge is as yourself. Spiritual realisation is similar. But instead of 'doing', you are 'being'. Unlike doing, being never ends. So the realisation of truth is like a drink that never ends. Every question, even ten or twenty years later, is answered with the same immediate certainty of knowledge, because the being or truth of the experience is still going on.

Due to my profound realisations, I am cosmically conscious. This means I am a conscious participant in the cosmic myth that is unfolding or revealing itself every moment in the divine mind, or cosmic space. I have direct knowledge of the origins of man and the universe and the purpose of life and death; of man's present status in the cosmic scheme and of what he must overcome, individually and as the race, before he can attain to cosmic consciousness.

However, despite all that I have said, I have still not told you the highest truth.

The highest truth is nothing.

This means that the highest truth can only be perceived when I-the-individual am as nothing: when I am at last free of trying to be or know something.

In that 'nothing' I then find something – that which every human heart longs for.

In the apparently nonsensical contradiction of what I have just said lies the impotent perplexity and sometimes fury of the westernised mind when it is faced with the truth. Its sole activity and its only strength lie in trying to be something or understand something, in trying to do something or know something. Whereas the truth is that to be yourself you must not be anything; and in order to know the peace that comes from knowing or understanding everything, you must know nothing.

The nothing that contains the peace or solution to everything, is God. Let me demonstrate this 'nothing', this aspect of God, to you.

When you are in the depths of unhappiness and feel that you can no longer go on, you are in the 'nothing'. It is terrible, awful. If you stay consciously and valiantly in that nothing – without trying to escape from it, because you realise that something more potently real is happening – you will eventually pass through it. Then the problem that caused you so much pain will not be able to afflict you again. You will have been freed, liberated from it, by God. Whereas the crises that you do not face properly and valiantly, in the dissolution of the nothing, are the ones that are still able to come back and hurt you.

The Virus of Division

Never the twain shall meet – except in Thee.

THERE IS A virus in the human brain. It's in a part of the brain that has evolved relatively recently, the perimeter devoted to western thought. The virus is rampant. Much dis-ease arises from it: emotionalism, unresolved guilt, discontent, highs and lows, sexual fantasy, self-doubt, senseless violence, adolescent uncertainty, wishful thinking, inexplicable fear – to name but a few.

The virus occurred and lives on at a point of division in the brain. This is the point where East meets West. Here western-ised thought tries, always in vain, to understand the sublime truth or being of the East. Such a meeting is impossible. As the poet Kipling said, 'East is East and West is West and never the twain shall meet'. It was the brainy effort of trying to bring about the impossible that caused, and still causes in the individual brain, a psychic reaction of inadequacy or rejection.

The East I refer to, and its truth of being, has nothing to do with the modernised East – which is part of the West. The truth and being of the East is in fact the undivided, original, pristine state of the brain, which remains always pure and untouched – despite the spread of the virus.

The virus is the almost irresistible demand to understand what is beyond understanding. The task of dying willingly to this demand is the means by which I enter and connect with the underlying purity and clarity of the brain. In this is the spirit realised – the spirit of the brain that has created and creates all.

35

The virus stimulates analysis and rationalisation. It ensures its survival in the brain by making divisions where there are none. This works well enough in the approach to material progress – which is what the virus substitutes in the outer world for man's conscious inner evolution, about which it is utterly ignorant. But as an approach to life and truth the progressive making of divisions is disastrous. The divisions become blocks of ignorance in the exposed brain.

The virus is like a bookmark I use to artificially separate a single text; to mark what I've read from what I haven't read. In spite of the importance of the division to me personally, it has no objective reality. The objective reality of my reading is the text, which remains single and whole as it always was. My division of it is purely subjective; and cannot be the truth since the position of the bookmark would vary with every reader. The truth of course is that the truth does not vary.

THE MYTH OF LIFE

The story of the earth is your own story.

THE 'MYTH OF LIFE', as I call it, is the true story of man as
the intelligence of the planet earth in the evolutionary
scheme of the cosmos. The myth is not fable. Nor is it just
another story. It is the means by which the truth can be told
and absorbed. True myth is the language that arises from the
formless, energetic, all-knowing unconscious deep within
you. The myth of life is your own story.

Many people on earth are now ready to hear and recognise
the mythic truth I have to tell. That is why it is being told.
The purpose is to help prepare man for his future role as a
cosmic being. This will require him to contribute to other
life in the cosmos the virtue unique to intelligent life on
earth.

The cosmic ethic of the earth is justice; whereas its global
ethic is acquisition. There is virtually no justice on earth
because of the worldwide materialistic consciousness of its
people.

There is no chance of justice being realised as a global way
of life in the time that is left for the world. For the masses it
must remain an ideal; meaning, nothing can be done about it,
because the masses do not want it. In this did Jesus, the
Buddha, Krishna and all the great masters fail.

No one can change the mass consciousness. But the
cosmic ethic of the earth can still be realised, made real, in

the individual. Only in himself can the individual succeed.

The evolutionary cosmic scheme is concerned with the whole of life before and after death as a continuum of consciousness. This is in direct contrast with the partial concept of a physical universe, fathered by scientific materialism which disregards the consciousness of the perceiver.

Planet earth is not a haphazardly-placed piece of rock and dirt in space. Events on earth are not a lucky dip. The planet is not just here to be used and misused as human intelligence sees fit. It is a cosmic ethic. It is essential to the scheme of the entire universe that the earth-ethic is made a sensory reality – an actual moral way of life.

Man's current fitness for this role is reflected in his treatment of men, women, children and all other life on the planet. As man is, so is his world. As he is, he has no idea what he's doing or what he's living for. He is a developing but immature intelligence, itching with discontent, cruelly competitive, arrogant in his crude self-determinism and infested with greed and violence – all arising from self-ignorance; so much so that now he does not know what to do to undo what he's done.

Man at present has only a personal, limited life. Being unworthy of cosmic life, he cannot discover other life in the universe – no matter how technically clever he becomes. At any time he can only be aware of the cosmic life that he has to get right now. At present, that is his own life on earth. Only when he gets that right will he discover other cosmic life; and then it will be his mature delight and life-purpose to help and guide it.

To be worthy of cosmic participation, man must free himself of his present condition. For this, he has to pass collectively, as the human race, through the living depths of his accumulated ignorance. What he has done unconsciously, he must realise consciously. He must experience the same isolation as all the forms of life he has selfishly abandoned and exploited. He must realise in himself (and as himself) the horror of the selfish world that he has afflicted on the beautiful earth. In this way man will learn to know himself as never before. These events will mark the end of the current era.

In the divine mind (the space or cosmos in which all happens) the part is as essential as the whole.

You, the individual man or woman, are as essential as the whole universe. You must get yourself right – now.

There is no point in thinking that death will do it for you, that you will die into a better world. There is no death: nothing changes fundamentally. The world you die into is no improvement on the one you leave, the one you made for yourself. You carry your world with you, in you. If you have not got it right on earth, you're not going to get it right anywhere else for long.

It is up to you. That is divine justice.

Time is the evolutionary process on this planet. In time, and on time, man will be truly intelligent – responsible life on earth. He will then make his unique contribution to the cosmic whole. He will know precisely what he is doing and the purpose of life on earth. He will be cosmically conscious and terrestrially mature. He will be a cosmic being.

This is the myth of life.

Are you hearing it?

Is it the truth for you?

The Love of Truth

Lose your passion for life and lose your way.

The energy of the myth of life, being the real story of our origins and intelligence and of all things, is so powerful that once heard it continues to work in the subconscious, even though the person may not be aware of it. The energy acts like a signal in anyone ready to listen. Each hearing triggers the release of a regenerative, spiritual impulse into the subconscious, where all man's false images and notions of himself and life are stored. He is reminded of the truth of himself and this reduces his attachment to the falsehoods.

As spiritual energy is formless it makes no impression on the memory. The person is unaware of anything happening – in terms of information. Nonetheless, the energy's purifying action is unmistakable. It is felt as a subtle delight or excitation in the region of the solar plexus.

Perhaps you have felt this? It is the beginning of passion, true passion – the love of truth or life that leads to the certainty of love found.

When man is deprived of the energy of true myth, as in the current electromagnetic epoch, he gradually loses touch with the fulfilling, self-moisturising substance of his own love within. Imperceptibly he dries up into an intellectualised mental being. For myth he substitutes rational thinking and scientific ideas. These merely describe his material and self-conscious condition and fail to signify any purpose, future or reality beyond his fleeting mundane existence and death. Mythically, as man loses his love he loses his way. When the individual loses his way he is forced to join the aimless wandering habit of the herd. This habit, the seasonal movement from one pasture to another while always covering the same old ground, man calls living, or progress.

I speak to the most intimate part of your being, the part of you that longs for love and truth. Since most people are not ready for love and truth, most people want entertainment, excitement, information and change – satisfaction. So they read newspapers, magazines and novels, watch television, listen to the radio and have interesting debates and discussions. We all enjoy these things to a degree. But when they are the main focus of our lives or of the people around us, we start to die inside. We dry up. Often, not knowing what's happening, we begin to think there's something wrong with us.

What has happened is that we have tired of the endless search for a satisfaction that never satisfies. We now want fulfilment, something lasting.

Love and truth are not information. Information is what is added to you, like all the data stored in your memory. Love and truth are knowledge – self-knowledge, original knowledge, the knowledge of the depths of your own being.

When I speak to you of love or truth I don't really tell you anything new. I merely reflect the knowledge of what you are, buried under all the information about what you think you are.

As this delights and fulfils you, it slowly brings you back to life.

How I Teach

I speak only of life, love, death, truth and God.

I TEACH OR reach you in two ways. By telling the myth of life I reach you through the intellect. The other way is through your emotional self, which is the more direct and painful way. You might have noticed the signs in yourself. If so, what's happening is that I am reaching you through your self.

You do not know the truth as I do. If you continue to listen to the truth I speak, then you must die every moment to any resistance rising in you; anything that wants to argue, be offended or slyly hold on to vague reservations. These are all emotional reactions, signs of residual tension or unhappiness in you. And it is this emotion – the ignorant insistence that you know the truth when you know you don't – that prevents you from seeing the truth every moment for yourself, without having to depend on someone else to point it out to you.

If you knew the truth you would never be unhappy. There can be no unhappiness, no tension, when you die now, this moment and every moment, to the false knowledge of yourself or life that you are holding on to, or are moved to defend.

Truth is reached by entering and descending into your subconscious through stillness and through listening to the words of the master. Only a master can get you there, someone who has gone before you through the subconscious and into the truth. He is like a guide who leads you down through the black maze of your fears, false conceptions and spurious emotions. Undeterred by your inevitable resistance and rebellious moods, he leads you onwards towards the truth, the beauty that is buried under your emotional and mental images of yourself.

This descent is actually taking place in you now, while you are reading.

The practice of self-discovery, as I teach it, deals in facts. It admits nothing to be true but that which is. No beliefs. Nothing to hold out a crutch. No authority to cite but the truth. Self-discovery dissolves and dissolves the falsehoods until nothing remains but what is true; and that is direct experience.

All realisation of life or truth comes direct, whereas living is 'indirect experience', in which no energy or knowledge comes to you straight. In indirect experience there is always 'this or that' – choice or wanting to choose. In direct experience there is no choice, no chooser. Direct experience is not dependent on your memory, imagination, emotions or even the idea that you have a body.

Your perception of your own truth or experience corresponds to your point of evolutionary development at any one time; and so is limited. But the limit can be penetrated, and then expanded, by contact with the right energy of a more realised truth.

I bring people to direct experience. This occurs when a person is sufficiently penetrated to expose a point of emotional congestion – the blockage causing the immediate confusion or ignorance. First the person's surface mind is penetrated to expose the blockage; then the deeper psyche, and finally its perimeter, beyond which lies limitless consciousness, the abstract field of intelligence, which is the unit and unity of direct experience.

This penetration, and its power, depends on love of the truth, passion for the truth. Passion is pure, mainstream. Emotion is a blockage in the stream.

An emotional blockage is commonly externalised by the questions a person asks. The question is the pain to know, the self-doubt, the discontent, the problem between the person and the immediate truth. This point of congestion is what must be penetrated, seemingly by words, in dealing with the question. In reality the words are symbols of the force (emotion) in the question and power (love) in the response. In other words, it is done energetically. The potential of the space between question and reply is polarised and becomes a unified field. Momentarily the questioner and I are poised in the one consciousness; communication is instantaneous and the blockage is temporarily or relatively cleared. For a brief instant the individual knows what he 'knows' – what he has always known but could not realise. This is the moment of direct experience.

Afterwards the questioner or seeker falls back into the confusion of his psyche, his world. There he (or she) will find another lump of complication and another question, if he can express it.

The process is the same, whether someone on the way to the truth asks me a question face to face, or is listening for the truth in reading my words.

Without right help we cannot realise what we know: we only think or assume we know. Realisation depends on right listening, right intelligence, right questions and sufficient penetration of right love and truth; so that every question, every doubt, is eliminated, not by suppression, belief or avoidance, but by the power of self-knowledge.

Though I may teach in groups, or speak to large audiences, I always speak to the individual. The level of penetration is different for each person; but the levels overlap, allowing one to learn from hearing the penetration of another.

I am concerned with the individual alone. The group, any group, becomes a blockage in the individual if he (or she) allows it to hold him. Only the energy that frees may hold; and then only as long as is absolutely necessary. The area of group experience is the psyche, where all energy is emotional. The group, like the masses, cannot share in the unity of consciousness – at least, not for many ages of evolution. Only the individual possesses that potential.

THE TRUTH OF THE MASTER

The master never dies.

MY TEACHING CONTAINS no dogma or ritual, requires no faith and follows no belief. It rests purely on the power of self-discovery. It invalidates all priests and middle-men. It is not for religionists and followers.

Since it is immediate and direct, this teaching reveals to the individual the essential truths of the founding masters of the world's great religions – all of whom knew themselves.

The truth of Christ is that Christ is not historical. Christ is now. Christ is an energy in the unconscious of man and woman at this moment. Christ is the ethic and living fragrance of the planet that arises from the essential idea of the Earth Spirit, the Father, at the foundation of the human psyche. Christ is resurrected now in every individual who is still enough inside to realise it.

Buddha is not historical either. Buddha is also now, an energetic presence in the human psyche. Buddha, or buddhi, is the pure unmoving intelligence that emerges from the deeper cosmic space of the divine unconscious, beyond even the psyche or the earth.

Historically, the Buddha born 600 years before Jesus represents the stillness of mind (the presence of intelligence) that had to be realised in an individual on earth before the Christ energy could be realised. All truth has to be lived and realised in man, by man on earth, for it to be the living truth and thus available to all men. For what one man has realised, all men in time can realise.

The master never dies. Nevertheless, men and women kill him by making him historical. They bury him under their own imaginings and deprive themselves of his ever-present power within. As the master disappears into the memory, beneath countless layers of human false-hoods (mostly engendered by priests), the power of his immediate energetic presence in the psyche is lost to consciousness; and the miracles cease. After the master's death an individual retaining the living presence of the master through love or union may indeed work miracles. But when priests start talking and blessing in the name of the master, they introduce the historical person and the power is lost.

While the master is physically present he discourages or destroys all attempts by followers to make the truth he is historical.

—'I am the way, the truth and the life, now. I am within you at this moment, not yesterday or tomorrow. Be the life that I am now, that same precious life that is in you now. Do not think about it. For what you think about is not it, not I. Take no thought, as the lilies of the field take none. I and the Father, life, am One: and you are my resurrection in the flesh – now.'

—'Nirvana is now as I am now; extinguished but never extinguishable. Erect no statues and make no drawings of me for what I am cannot be seen or represented. The buddhic truth I am, the enlightenment I am, is now. Be poised and unwavering in the thoughtless mind now, and not in some future life. That is right action; and it will keep you beyond the delusion of desire and ignorance.'

Today, when a man or woman is 'born again', which seems to be a phenomenon of the West, the veil of ignorance in the subconscious is partly torn away – revealing the power of presence of the master, the truth, the word, the teaching that was always there.

You will not find the truth of the master in interpretations by well-intentioned disciples or followers.

Priests, due to the habit they put on, do not know the truth.

You must go to the words of the master himself. His word alone carries the ultimate power or truth – now. Do not compromise with relative, indirect, time-taking forces. Go for the ultimate, the power itself.

Be still and listen to the master until you become the truth, the stillness, that he is.

THE WAY OF STILLNESS

You discover yourself in stillness.
Stillness is introduced through right meditation.
Right meditation is discovering
what you are now;
not what you have been or think you are.

MEDITATION

The way to the light.

'WHY DO I need to meditate?'

To know yourself.

'Why do I need to know myself?'

Because what you are at present, what you think you are, is not yourself. That's why you are never really content for long: you know unconsciously you are not yourself. Consequently, you often feel insecure, uncertain and even afraid.

Inside you is a wonderful, helpful, loving and uniquely creative being. You know it, at least sometimes. But that loving, creative 'you' is very difficult to externalise and bring into the world. Too often your finest intentions and feelings are misinterpreted and misunderstood. So you become discontented again and unhappy with yourself.

We start off life with such splendid dreams and intentions. We're all innocent to begin with. Do we really lose that innocence? No. We just allow it to become covered over. The world has a way of bringing the worst out of each of us, turning us into what we once were not. We gather the world. Layer by layer we silt ourselves up and are enclosed by a subtle and insidious accretion. There's this dark, false side of ourselves that we've subconsciously allowed to build up over the years; and that is the trouble.

There is a light at the end of the tunnel and that is what's pulling you on. It is what brought you to this moment. It is the truth of yourself, the 'real you' that you have become separated from. The meditation I teach is the tunnel back through the gloom.

So, meditation, as I teach it, is a way to discover the truth of yourself. You are wasting your time if you don't want to know the truth; if you don't want to know yourself as you really are; if you are not willing to start facing up to yourself.

Right meditation – and not all meditation methods are right – is a total way towards healthy living. It dissolves the muck of the world in you. The muck of the world is time – time the world has finished with. The time that is here now, every moment, is no problem. But the time that has gone, the past that you cling to as the memory of yourself, your life, the past you won't let go of, that is the waste of time.

The sheer weight of the past makes you and everyone else psychologically old, burdened, while you are still physically young. It forces you to constantly think or talk about the past. This makes you doubt yourself in the present – which is fear and worry.

Where else but in the memory of the past does the sadness and loneliness come from that makes you so often have to pretend and put on a brave face? What has happened to the carefree days when you used to feel alive and vibrant without having to try? Why is living so often tedious? And why does love, so simple and delightful at first, inevitably turn into a non-event, a pain or a problem?

You have gathered too many yesterdays. You are loaded with past. Day by day, year in and year out, as subtly as dust gathers on a polished table, you've allowed the past with all its unsolved problems, hurts and disappointments to accumulate. And now it has fastened on to you like a hard dead skin you cannot shed. Painfully, you are attached to it.

The meditation I teach brings you into the present. Gradually you start to come alive. You grow psychologically younger.

Once more you begin to savour the beauty of the earth and the life and love on it.

This is not just a method to help you sit regularly in silence and stillness. It opens the way into yourself. It is a continuous unfoldment of the way into your being, to where you are eternally young because the cramping past, the vast waste of time, has finally been left behind.

GOING WITHIN

Through the barriers of thought.

MEDITATION IS THE art of entering your own unconscious.

Your unconscious – where the truth of yourself lies – is inside your body. It is a place of extraordinary stillness and creativity. When you reach it you will know that learning to meditate was the most important move you ever made.

Everything you are is inside your body. But penetrating to the level of the unconscious is not easy. The unconscious is three levels down. If you imagine an underground carpark, the top level, street level, is the conscious where you are now. The second level is the subconscious, where all your thoughts come from. The third level is the unconscious. So going down, you have to pass through the subconscious to get to the unconscious. And the subconscious, which is a sort of guardian to the lower level, is going to do all it can to deflect and distract you by throwing up a screen of thoughts.

To meditate successfully, all unnecessary thinking eventually has to stop. By unnecessary thinking I mean aimless use of the memory. For example, when you're sitting doing nothing the mind tends to wander all over the place. Not because you need to think about those particular topics but because the mind, when it's not concentrated, has got into the wandering habit; and you probably never thought to try to stop it.

Stopping thinking is a gradual process and not an easy one. But you can make a start by accepting that when you sit down to meditate, there is not one thought that can come into your mind that is valid. You are there to meditate. You don't have to think about your worldly affairs, paying the rent, posting a letter or what train you've got to catch. If you feel you do, go ahead and think about it. And then come back to your meditation.

Eventually you will have to master the subtle, cunning thinker who has been controlling your mind for so long without you realising it. And when you do, you'll sail through into the amazing stillness of the vast unconscious – the truth of yourself.

If you think or want to argue that it's impossible to stop thinking, please don't. That has been said to me so many times before. And so many times have I heard and seen the amazement of people who started out just like you and burst suddenly into that incredible stillness and space within themselves.

For yourself, you should know that I have penetrated the unconscious to its deepest level. I am in the unconscious now. If I weren't there I would be giving you secondhand information and instructions I'd picked up from someone else. For I do not just inform you of the techniques of meditation. Using the energy of my discovered unconscious, I actually take you down into yourself where you have never consciously been before.

The more attention you give to what I say and the more you put into practice the meditation I teach, the more you are able to consciously enter the unconscious where I am. That is what meditation is for.

But meditation is a process of self-unfoldment and cannot be rushed. It must be done bit by bit. And it must be done there – in your body.

START MEDITATING NOW

*Are you willing to come with me
to a new place within yourself?*

LET US LOOK at the resources at our disposal. First there is
your body. That is what you are going to enter. Please look
down at it.

Look down at it now.

What are you using to look with?

Your attention. Your attention is the other part of you. It is
the instrument you use to enter the body.

Where your attention is at any time is where you are as a
perceiving individual. For 99.9 per cent of our lives, our
attention is centred on the external reality, the world. It is
going out of our body, away from the inner reality. By
meditating, we are deliberately attempting to break down
that imbalance in ourselves. We are endeavouring to turn our
attention inward, into the body where the subconscious and
deeper unconscious realities are located. These have been
greatly neglected. That neglect shows in man's lopsided and
unsatisfying materialistic view of life and his preoccupation
with progress, which is mostly all external and unrelated to
his inner self.

After millions of evolutionary years focusing on the external
world, we are going to be kicking a monolithic habit. So
don't be discouraged if thoughts keep distracting your attention. Even in the early stages, however, you will get some

brief moments of stillness and thoughtlessness, and that will convince you that what you are attempting is worthwhile. Each time discursive thought stops, you'll feel more yourself, more steady and more in control. And when you see that for an instant the mind did stop, do not doubt it. It will be true. But you mustn't think about it. Just accept it, and it will happen again and again, with a little more conviction each time.

It's important to remember this: when you feel you've had an unusual inner experience, do not doubt it.

So let's start meditating now.

First, sit erect on a chair with your feet together on the floor, unless you're accustomed to sitting cross-legged, eastern style.

Don't loll: you're likely to go to sleep. Remember, we go to sleep each night by withdrawing into our subconscious and the attempt to enter the body consciously, as we are doing now, is likely to be taken by the body as a command to go to sleep.

So sit up straight.

Now we want you, your attention, to go inside the body. We must stop you going outside it. We must close the main portholes of escape – your eyes. I would ask you to close your ears too, if that were possible. So please put the book aside for a few minutes. Close your eyes, sit up straight and see if you can actually put your attention on the eyeballs themselves. See how long you can stay there before you start thinking.

The next step is to take a few deep breaths.

The body tends to get tense in any situation in which something new or difficult is being tackled. You breathe more quickly and shallowly, leaving yourself short of air and your blood short of oxygen. The result is restlessness of body and mind: the subconscious starts furiously throwing up thoughts, giving you no chance of getting into yourself.

In this meditation, you quieten the body by taking a special kind of breath, down into the lower part of the lungs, an area that normally gets very little aeration.

This is what you do. First, you breathe out. You empty your lungs as completely as you can. You don't want to start meditating on old air. Squeeze it all out, using the muscles in the rib-cage. It can help to bend forward a little to expel the last of the air.

Then you breathe in as slowly and gently as you can. Breathe the air in deeply, directing it towards your stomach. It is as if you are aiming to fill your belly with air and not your chest. Your diaphragm will expand. But as soon as the chest begins to lift, you stop. This is very important: stop the in-breath when the chest starts to rise.

Next you hold the breath – just for a few seconds, before breathing out again as slowly as you can. Once you are used to it, you can hold the breath a little longer but not so as to overdo it or distress the body.

When you have filled your lungs and are holding your breath, you can push the air down towards the lower abdomen. Use the muscles of the back and the rib-cage to 'bear down' like women do in childbirth. Push the air down and move it around for three or four seconds. Then release it as slowly as you can.

What you are doing is opening up the lower part of your lungs, oxygenating the blood and revitalising the entire respiratory system. The extra oxygen makes some people feel a bit dizzy sometimes. I emphasise that you must not distress your body in any of this. Do not force it or overdo it. Moderation is best.

When you sit down to meditate, take three or four of these breaths. And whenever you find yourself distracted or thinking it is a sure sign you need a few more deep breaths.

Eventually you will find you do not have to give any attention to your breathing – because the body breathes easily and naturally from the diaphragm, as it did when it was a baby.

The body is quiet. You are sitting erect. Now you are going to take your attention back out of the world around you and put it inside your body.

I suggest you read through the next few paragraphs, then close your eyes and put what I am saying into practice.

First, put your attention on the area around the eyes – the eyeballs, the eyelids, the area at the back of the eyes. You may notice your eyelids flickering a little as you do this. Then put your attention between the eyebrows.

With your eyes closed, look at the back of the eyelids. Then look up.

With practice, you will find there is a point there where the attention gathers. It locks in there with a feeling of rightness. Sometimes it can be a tension. Or there may be a feeling of release. Some people get to this point quickly: others take longer. The thing to remember is that this is where you gather yourself at the beginning of meditation.

Now close your eyes and practise that before reading further.

Next you direct the attention onto the feeling in your hands. With eyes closed, look down through your body and see what's going on in the hands – inside them. Don't visualise their external form: perceive the energy of them.

What is the sensation? Do this and find out what it feels like.

Take your time. Be easy and relaxed. Take a deep breath, with a gentle inhalation, and breathe out slowly.

In the same way as you go and find the sensation in your hands, you can go to other parts of the body. It is always different, always new. At the beginning it may seem a bit like pins and needles – a sort of tingling. The sensation gets finer as you give more of your attention to it.

So go around the body with your attention. Start with the lips. They are very sensitive. The sensation there is very fine. And while your attention is there, lift the corners of the lips into a smile. Do this deliberately. People often look unduly serious in meditation – a bit down in the mouth; perhaps it's the feeling of concentration that does it. Rightly done, meditation is a joyous, relaxing and restoring activity. By lifting the lips a little, you actually set in motion the lighter energies of the face. These tend to rise up naturally towards the eyes and make a real smile – a lightening of attention, a release of tension.

While your attention is on the face, focus on the tip of the nose. There's a very distinct sensation there. And what is the sensation of your tongue like?

Go around the body and explore the sensations for yourself. Go to the feet. The knees. The small of the back. The shoulders. The back of the neck.

What can you feel in each of these places? Tingling? Pulsing?

In this way you bring yourself to life. You are developing another sense, an inner sense. I call this inner way of perceiving 'apperception'. That is to distinguish it from normal perception which uses the external senses. Normally we apperceive only when we have a pain. Pain is not just a warning device. It's an attempt by the organism to draw our attention inward; but man has lost the knack of using pain in this constructive way.

You must familiarise yourself with your body apperceptively and do so as often as you can remember. Don't wait until you are sitting in meditation. At any time of the day you can practise. Just put your attention into different parts of the body and see what the sensation is.

Now give yourself a little time to sit in silence. Commit yourself by accepting that there is nothing else you have to do. Check your posture. Take your breaths. Gather your attention in. Be still.

Start meditating now.

THE RELEASE OF TENSION

Be without trying to be.

THE NEXT STEP is to learn to release the tension that you are continuously building up in the body; and which, unsuspected, is creating tomorrow's headache or irritability.

You are continuously wasting some of your finest energy by putting unnecessary effort or tension into simple activities. Take, for example, the way you use your eyes. Are you aware of how much energy is going out through your eyes in the effort of concentration?

Stop reading for a moment and just look at the number of this page. Thirty seconds will do.

Now look at the number a second time. This time take the effort and the concentration out of looking. Pull back behind the eyes. Relax the forehead. Allow the corners of the lips to rise.

Did you notice the difference?

This is something you can practise often and in many situations. Take the tension out of looking. Pull back until you can see out of the corners of your eyes. Look peripherally. Blink to cut out the concentration and the staring.

The same principle applies to the hearing. Pull back out of the ears, relaxing the effort you use to hear. Release the strain of it.

The problem is that we humans have got into the habit of projecting ourselves out through our eyes, ears and skin, and to a less discernible degree through the other senses. The senses were evolved to receive information, not to project it. Part of your meditation is to reverse this habit of self-projection. And of course the energy you save is the very energy you need to go within.

So every time you can think of it during the day, pull back from the eyes and see without looking; listen without needing to hear.

In fact, be without trying to be. Make this the first step towards taking the trying out of your life. When you give up trying, you don't stop seeing, hearing, sensing, being or doing: your performance is just less wearying and more as nature intended.

Where do you feel tense, strained? What parts of your body are tight?

It might be that you feel something like a band of energy around your head, or a weight across your shoulders.

Close your eyes and take a look around inside. Look for inner tension. Whenever you find any, you endeavour to release it by 'dropping it down'.

If there is any tension in the upper part of the body, you put your attention on it and let the tension fall down into the lower abdomen. This is the natural garbage pit of the body. Everything not needed by the organism ends up here, where it can be dealt with and dissolved; and that should include any stress you consciously face up to and deal with in this way.

You drop the tension down by surrendering it, by giving it up, by not holding on to it a moment longer.

Now move the attention around the body again. Go into the shoulders. That's one of the easiest places to feel tension because we all tend to store it there. Go to the back of the neck; another place where there is often a tightness or tension that has risen up from the shoulders.

Drop it all down.
Let it drain down towards the stomach.
You don't want the tension do you?
Then give it up.

THE WELL OF BEING

Stop holding on to your life.

WHAT YOU ARE endeavouring to do is learn a simple art: how to desist from unconsciously using your attention to hold on to your body.

Tension is unconscious attention. As soon as you make the unconscious attention conscious, the tension around it dissolves and disappears.

Most people are holding on to their body like grim death, with unconscious fingers of tension. You have to give that up and learn to surrender this fear-full hold you have on yourself.

The following exercise will help you. It is a most important technique and you should make it a regular part of your meditation practice.

You have closed your eyes. You have put your attention on the sensation of the body.

Your body is a well.

You don't know how deep the well is, only that you are not at the bottom.

You are supporting yourself from falling any further by pushing out against the sides of the well.

You can feel the tension of holding on.

Why are you holding on?

What are you holding on to?

It's only yourself – the well of yourself.

Let go a little. Relax.

Slip down into the darkness, into the unknown.

As you get used to it, it becomes quite pleasant.

The well is very, very deep. It is your depth. As that depth you are unfathomable.

Don't be anxious about slipping down further than you can handle. You can relax completely because your tension not only keeps you from the depths of yourself but also protects you from dropping down too quickly. Trust yourself.

Give up.

Let go.

Surrender.

THE ENERGY OF THE SPINE

Be still in the presence of power.

WHAT THE HINDUS call the kundalini or shakti power is the creative energy of nature – the life force – which culminates in us as the sex drive. Before differentiating into sexual desire it is an extremely pure energy and, though dormant, it is located at the bottom of the spine. We are likely to tap into it in meditation, as we descend deeper into the unconscious. The effect can be dramatic both physically and psychologically.

Physically, the energy travels swiftly up the back, compulsively straightening the spine and pulling the head back. The eyeballs may tend to roll up towards the forehead. The energy may be felt spreading over the crown of the head and coming to a point between the eyebrows. This is the identical point that I suggested you focus your inner attention on whenever you begin to meditate. The idea is to help to encourage the awakening of this kundalini-shakti power.

The psychological effect of the power is extraordinarily elevating and enlightening. There is no mistaking that you are experiencing something outside the norm of everyday data. You are aware of intensified conscious intelligence, or will, working in you or taking over your being or body. In no sense is it felt to be harmful or a violation of your individuality. It is usually a brief experience and it may not occur again. But the eminently positive effects of profound clarity, understanding or love may continue for days or even weeks afterwards.

Another phenomenon likely to be encountered in meditation at some time is psychic energy. Unlike the kundalini-shakti power this is not desirable in itself. Psychic energy is a force that tends to intrude and distract rather than assist in the journey towards the truth of yourself.

Sometimes in meditation you may feel your body starting to quiver imperceptibly. This is a sign of the kundalini power trying to rise up the spine and as such is progressive. But it is the nature of psychic energy to try to fasten on to any expression of power or spirit – such as kundalini activity. So you have to avoid allowing the quiver to become a sway or develop into anything like a side-to-side pendulum movement. Pronounced swaying will generate more psychic energy and you will find yourself distracted; with the likely result that you will become stuck in this spiritually unproductive area.

Remember, what you are endeavouring to do is to become stiller so as to sink deeper into yourself and release the uplifting and unifying energies. Psychic energy is counter-productive of stillness. It excites curiosity, speculation and superstition, which is the very turbulence we are aiming to sink down through.

How will you know when you reach the bottom of yourself? There'll be no mistaking this rare experience when it happens. But an indication that you are approaching it is when you feel a fine pins-and-needles sensation in your belly, and it is as though that sensation is your whole body – the sensation of any other part vanishes and all you have is the one sensation, as though you don't have a physical body at all.

DROPPING THE HABIT

*How to gain energy
through intelligent self-observation.*

THOUGH YOU ENDEAVOUR to sink down into yourself,
sometimes your heartbeat and breathing may distract you and
prevent you from going deeper. The mind fixes itself on the
heart or the breathing and you remain stuck there until the mind
tires of its fixation. Getting past these two (especially the heartbeat, which often becomes very noticeable when you're trying
to go to sleep at night) depends a good deal on overcoming
the mind's habitual curiosity. The mind is always looking for
something to latch on to, inside or outside. And that brings us
to the next stage in your meditation or way to stillness.

Meditation is not just a matter of entering your body.
That's only half of it. The other half involves becoming more
conscious of the way you perform and react to the world.

Take the habit of useless curiosity. Say you are walking down
the street and someone behind shouts in a loud voice. Everyone
looks around. Why? —Only because of habit or curiosity.

Did you really think the shout was for you? No. You just
turned around without being aware of what you were doing.
And if you turned out of curiosity, why did you need to know
what was going on?

Similarly, if there is an accident and a curious crowd is
gathering, why should you want to join in to witness or know
about another's misfortune?

By participating in this so-called 'harmless' curiosity you give the mind the power to distract you.

Another helpful exercise is to refuse to count the chimes of a clock – while still hearing them. The mind, you will notice, automatically counts the strikes.

Also, when people are conversing around you and you're not involved, such as in a doctor's waiting room or a bus, try letting the words pass through your head without translating them. This all helps to give you control over your mind.

We are all creatures of habit. But some habits are more useless and waste more energy than others. It's those that we want to rid ourselves of, so that we can use the energy more effectively to find ourselves. And we do it by intelligent observation of our own useless habits.

From this moment on you must become more aware of your involuntary physical actions. You have to name them for yourself. You might be someone who habitually wastes energy by allowing your fingers to drum on the desk, or who fiddles with things, taps your foot, talks aimlessly, makes phone calls that have no real purpose, and so on. In short, endeavour to stay aware and put a stop to some of these unconscious and habitual actions. You'll discover plenty of ground for habit-breaking.

WORRYING

The penalty for having thought.

WE ACCEPT SOME things in ourselves as harmless or natural because we haven't looked at them intelligently. They are often behind our negative moods and depressions. Take worry, for instance. Nothing is more punishing and destructive than worry. Yet worry is only another name for undisciplined thinking.

Worry is the penalty for imagining that thinking is harmless or natural.

Let me explain, for this is crucial to your new peace of mind. To worry is to be unable to stop thinking about a matter that's disturbing you. If you could stop thinking about it, you wouldn't be worried. You might still feel a kind of background heaviness, or a dull ache, but the pain behind the worry only recurs when you touch it with thinking and remember it.

The question, of course, is how can you possibly stop thinking when you're worried?

The way is to gradually get control of the thinker in you and this means, first of all, making the effort to give up thinking when you are not worried.

From now on, resolve not to think about what you did yesterday or even five minutes ago. You will not think about what you said, where you went, what you saw, what someone else said. In other words, give up thinking about the past as self-amusement.

You cannot expect to stop thinking in bad times (which is worry) if you allow your mind the same freedom to think in good times. Even to lie in bed thinking about a movie or a play you've just seen, or a lovely day out with a friend, is to encourage the mind to do precisely the same thing when next you have a problem, and then it will keep you awake with worry.

So, no more day-dreaming. No more thinking about the good times – or the bad times.

All worry is tension: all thinking is a form of tension. As you go on giving it up in all the ways I've mentioned you will be going deeper into yourself, thinking less about the past and living more in the present.

EMOTIONAL RELATIONSHIPS

*If you think, then you must drink
at the place of the sinking heart.*

EVERY TIME YOU have a row or argument you may notice that the emotion of it lingers in your stomach below the solar plexus. The emotion is like a continuation of the dispute inside you and it forces you to think over and over all that was said, as well as a lot that wasn't but you wish you'd said. Frequently the emotion makes you fabricate a completely new and favourable dialogue with which you tease and entertain yourself.

From now on, if you are serious in your self-discovery, you have to make more constructive use of such situations. They have to be treated as opportunities to get to know yourself better, to clear out the nonsense and to go deeper down into the unconscious.

This is what you do; and it is a most important exercise. Next time you have a row, resist as much as possible the urge to think about what has happened. Unless thought is necessary to help you take action, by thinking you are merely playing emotional games and indulging yourself. Unless you intend to act on the thought, there is no excuse whatever for thinking; and certainly not for brooding.

So next time you have a row, go somewhere on your own, and sit down if you can. Treat it as a meditation. Gather yourself between the eyebrows. Take several deep, long, diaphragmatic breaths: they are crucial on these occasions.

Now centre your attention on the emotion in your stomach. This will help to keep the mind occupied, as it will be straining to think.

Hold the emotion by examining the sensation of it – just as you learned to hold and identify the tingling sensation in the other parts of your body.

Each time you catch yourself thinking, start again. Take more deep breaths; don't allow the chest to rise. And go straight back to the emotion in your stomach.

Don't think. Hold the emotion. Enter it. Be the emotion. Suffer it. Be the pain. Groan if it helps. But don't try to escape it by thinking. Don't walk around. Don't move.

Bear it as long as you can. You have to rid yourself of this alien thing by confronting it, burning it out of you. If you think about it, talk about it or move because of it, you are running from it – running from the discomfort and pain.

Don't be fooled; it is using you. You can get rid of it this way, get rid of it forever. If you don't face up to it now (most people don't) it will be back tomorrow, next month or next year to torment and agonise you again. Only by then it will have joined up with all your other unresolved emotional conflicts, and will make you feel more wretched and miserable.

It's because we don't face up to emotions that we accumulate all negative feelings, as well as those deadening dark layers of false self that I mentioned earlier. After each emotional blow we deaden or desensitise a part of ourselves so we won't feel the pain as severely next time. And of course the self-protective crust that builds up has the side-effect of making us feel enclosed and cut off from the vibrancy of life.

Can you see how important it is to face up to your emotion?

By using the attention to hold the sensation of the emotion you gradually dissolve it. By refusing to think you actually starve it, deny it life. Think, and you immediately revive it.

Isn't that true? Check it next time you've got an emotional crisis on your hands. It hurts only when you remember it by thinking about it.

Go into meditation now. Place your attention on the stomach area and find out what you are feeling there.

See if there's a disturbance or something distracting you. If there is, it's a relationship to something outside yourself.

Is it something in the past? Or something in the future? A demand made on you by someone? Or by yourself?

Place your attention upon it and continue in meditation for as long as you can hold the sensation – or until it dissolves.

RELEASING YOUR PRISONERS

Let them go. Be emptied.

AFTER YOU'VE HAD some success at handling your emotions, the next exercise follows almost naturally. But it will only work for you after you've made meditation, or the search for truth, a high priority in your life.

There are now locked up inside of you, as in a jail, a number of people. They are your psychological prisoners. Although they give you a great deal of trouble, you are afraid to let them go.

These are people you've been attached to, where emotion has entered the relationship; mother, father, boss, wife, husband, children, former lovers, old school chums and the like. Whether alive or dead, still in contact or apparently forgotten, they live on in you as emotional entities. If you see, think or dream about one of them, depending on the intensity of the relationship, up pops the old energy of the person or situation and you are emotionally disturbed again. These emotions are searingly real in their effect on you. And yet they are phantoms.

You have to release these emotional prisoners. This is what you do . . .

Sit in meditation in the ordinary way. Take some breaths. Gather your attention and lift the corners of the lips. Then put the attention on the abdomen. Your specific intention is to free 'anyone', to release any negative feeling against another that you might have locked up inside of you as a result of the past.

For example, it might be the feeling that your mother or father 'failed' you at some time in your life. Let's say it's your father. Let the feeling go. Smile. Let him go. Forgive him with love – not necessarily love for him, but just love or goodwill. See that all you've been holding on to was your own self-centred expectation of what a father should be. If he was not a good father, so what? It's all behind you: all the more reason not to hold on to him. The truth is he owed you nothing that he did not give. He gave what he could, all that his nature and conditioning allowed – just as you give. Any failure or denial was only life, your life at that time, which you can now let go of.

Liberate 'anyone', any feeling inside of resentment or grudge towards another. Name the person. Free them of any further demands from you. Say, 'I free you in love from any debt or blame I may have been holding over you. You owe me nothing.'

The problem or person inside you is felt as a sort of tension, tightness or pressure. You can actually open up or unlock the tension. Feel it opening up. Feel the resentment slipping out – not with a looking back, but with the joy of freedom. Feel the prisoners going in love – free at last of your holding and concealing.

If you find any emotional entities trying to stay around, shoo them away by inwardly saying, 'Be free. Be gone. There is nowhere left here for you to hide. I am empty, emptied.'

Do all this with a sense of love, of giving. You are returning all that you ever held back; becoming more and more emptied and transparent.

By giving and loving in this way you are surrendering your old self, your old deadening emotional layers. You are being made new, fresh, alive.

THE PIGMY

Now you must tackle the enemy within.

I'M GOING TO tell you about the 'pigmy' that lives in each one of us. This is a little man or woman, a dwarfish and ugly part of each of us, a cunningly intelligent entity, stunted, tricky, shifty and knowing. If I call him 'he' and you are a woman, you must call him 'she'.

The pigmy is no stranger to you. You might feel it's something I've dreamed up to make a point, but it's as real as you are and in some ways your oldest friend.

The pigmy is the living past in you. You probably thought the past had gone like yesterday. But it hasn't; not the past that caused you any emotional pain. That past lives on in you now as the pigmy. It consists of every disappointment since you were a child, every secret hurt, unfulfilled expectation, every unfounded assumption about life and living that wounded you. In other words, the pigmy is the lie or compromise you have allowed yourself to live, or were forced to live, when the truth of that emotional moment or situation should have been found by you, or explained to you. That small, dark body of accumulated emotional energy which has never been intelligently examined – your ignorance – is alive in you as the pigmy.

The pigmy is responsible for all your negative moods, fears, doubts, depression and unhappiness. He is the falseness of your self.

Do you recognise him, or her?

The pigmy is also the glutton in you. If you want to meet him then observe yourself the next time you are greedy for food, sex, drink, recognition, love, respect or anything. Try pulling back from your greed, or walking away, and you'll soon feel the pigmy's fury. He'll quickly justify your appetite; and debunk what I'm saying now as nonsense. But after he's had his fill – that is, after the particular moment of truth is passed, and you are left despondent and disliking yourself – you will know that what I'm saying is true. You cannot deceive yourself; you know when you've failed yourself – when the pigmy has won. The deceit is in choosing to ignore the intelligence in you who sees the truth.

It is the pigmy that wants the last word in an argument, and justifies that need.

It is the pigmy that fantasises about sex, using your memory to do so.

It is the pigmy that wallows in thinking about grievances, insults and revenge; again using your memory.

The pigmy lives in the memory. It is he that does all your thinking about the past, the good times and the bad. Stop thinking and he's practically homeless.

The pigmy thrives on emotional excitement, good or bad. And he doesn't care about consequences. After he's indulged himself in the world, he leaves you to clean up the mess and cope with the inner traumas. You might have noticed.

Mastering the pigmy is a continuous exercise, a battle which in the end you have to win. But when you fail in an encounter with him, don't despair. Before long you'll have another opportunity to observe the way he uses you; another opportunity to withdraw from him if you can.

The pigmy can't indulge himself without you. He has no physical body, only an emotional one, and no memory of his own, so he uses yours and feeds off you.

The pigmy doesn't like the idea of you entering yourself. He may go along with your meditation for a while, but when he finds that you are really serious he'll fight furiously to keep you from putting the spotlight of intelligence, your attention, on him.

Have you felt any pains while you were meditating? A sudden headache perhaps? Or an unusual restlessness or resentment towards me? That was the pigmy, fearful and threatening. He is the only real enemy.

The way of truth and stillness that I teach is the beginning of the end of the pigmy. Nevertheless he is at his fiercest and meanest when cornered. He will play on every weakness, especially doubt. He will undermine your faith and confidence when you are in fact doing well. And if he can, he'll persuade you to give up meditation and self-discovery altogether.

I trust you persevere. Take every opportunity you can to hold the pigmy at bay.

DOING IT FOR LIFE

What is made in time is dissolved in time.

HOW OFTEN AND for how long should you meditate? To begin with, at least twice a day and for at least 15 minutes a sitting; preferably before you go to work and when you come home. You'll gradually get into a routine of your own. But be careful that it doesn't become another habit. Vary the times. There's no reason why, if you have the time, you shouldn't sit and meditate six times a day, for as long as you like. The important thing is not to put it off.

Just as important as sitting, is remembering to practise the other techniques, such as habit breaking and not thinking about the past.

It will take time learning to apply what I have shown you. A period of some years may be necessary for you to master each stage, in your own time. And then you can move on. A sense of urgency is valuable but there should be no sense of rush.

It may help you absorb what I have been teaching in this part of the book if you also listen to the tape-recorded version of it. [See Notes pp 298-9]. As you listen to my speaking voice you absorb the energy of what I am saying. I can take you into yourself as you listen. My other books and tapes will also help you at different stages of the process.

Be prepared for it to take time to get results. Remember to return to what I have said and written, because there will be things you read today that will not be meaningful or practical for you until you read them again at another time.

Get accustomed to using the inner feeling of your body to tell you what is going on in you at any moment. No more waiting for a pain or a twinge to discover you've got a thriving inner reality. Your body within is a very sensitive receiving apparatus. But you've got to learn how to get in there and read it.

Any time you feel a tightness or heaviness in your stomach you must not ignore it: it means something. You must apperceive what relationship is causing it. Then you must confront it. You will find that any tension or agitation in the stomach (apart from pain with a physical cause) has a crossed relationship with someone or something behind it. Search out the relationship. Be honest. Don't cover up. Name it to yourself. Once you know the origin of an emotion you feel less disturbed, less in the dark. And often you'll then see it to be so trivial that the disturbance just disappears.

Gradually meditation will become a total life activity for you, in which the vital stillness of your being will be constantly accessible. This is because meditation puts you back in contact with life. People confuse life with living, but life and living, remember, are two different things. Life is the earth. Living is the world.

Living is the superstructure that we, as humanity, have erected on life, on ourselves. Living is hard; at its best, not easy. Living is trying to cope with the world – an impossibility: we all compromise to get by. Living is compromise, is settling for the best you think you can obtain.

Life on the other hand is beautiful. Life begins with nature and ourselves. You don't have to compromise with life. It's just there, in you and around you. Life is all that is beautiful and natural. The trouble is we've got into the habit of thinking that living is natural. Living is not natural. That's what makes it so darned difficult.

You are only unhappy when you're trying to contend with living. You don't have to compromise or make allowances to hear the birds, to see the beauty of the trees, the sky, the grass, the animals around you. To be alive you just have to 'be'.

Total life is love. When you're in love, you're not worried about what the world might or might not do to you. You couldn't care less. While you are in love, you are in contact with life and you are alive. But unfortunately love at present is only a very small part of living.

No talk of truth or finding yourself is complete without love. Love is the final word. A life of self-discovery and stillness has to be accompanied by a growing awareness of love. Because love is only a giving up of your old dead self.

When you're sitting in silence and hear a bird singing, allow the sound to enter your solar plexus or stomach area; connect with it. It is fresh with life and will help to put you in touch with the love of life within you.

Also, you must endeavour to love more in the world. It is not enough for you to say you love someone or something. That allows you to regard love as a static, finished thing, whereas love is an intensely active, ceaseless state of being. So know or say 'I love you' – and then finish with: 'but I must love you more.' In that active commitment you will grow in love and life.

THE WAY OF LOVE

How do you love God?
You start by getting to know yourself
and by learning to love one another
as man and woman.

A WAY OF LOVE FOR THE WEST

You must face the truth of sexual love.

I AM GOING to present to you, men and women of this world, a new way to truth and enlightenment – the way of human sexual love, one for another.

Several ways to truth and divine fulfilment have come down to us through the centuries. The best known are probably the ways of the Buddha and Jesus. The way of the Buddha is for those extraordinary people who, like Gautama Buddha 2,500 years ago, can manage to master the mind, and the desires behind it, until it is reduced to the stillness of pure intellect and reveals all. The way of Jesus is the way to truth and divine union through self-sacrificing love of your neighbour or mankind. Men like Jesus and the Buddha are rare among us. This serves to show how little these ways are understood, how difficult they are for the ordinary individual to relate to and actually follow. But each of you can understand the love or need of a mate – for it comes from your deepest ache.

The ways of Jesus and the Buddha came out of the East. The way of man and woman as love, one for another, also comes out of the East – out of the original East which had vanished long before the birth of Gautama or Jesus. All lasting good derives from the original East which, although far removed in time, remains a sublimely potent point deep in the human unconscious.

Even so, this way of man and woman may be called a way for the West, a way of love for our loveless times, a gift from the beginning of time for those of you of today who can hear.

This way is no easier than the other ways. But at least it does not require you to meditate under a Bo tree for a year. Or die for your fellow man. And as I outline this way you will notice that the quality of it is consonant with your first expectations of love – before they were brutalised by the world's concepts of it.

This is a spiritual teaching of love; meaning it takes you back to the beginning of love on earth and then returns you to the present, where love is made now.

All love comes through physical love. The celibate saint who loves God, and may feel incapable of physical love, came out of physical, sexual love.

Love that avoids or ignores the ground of love between man and woman – each other's bodies – is intellectual love. The truth is that there is no love in the intellect, only the concept of it. To the intellect, love is a belief. But real love, like God, is beyond belief.

Unless you learn how to make right physical love you cannot really love your fellow man or woman.

It is here on earth where there is so little love, that love needs to be made. And if you can't make it – which means your love-life is unhappy or you have turned your back on physical love – you have turned away from love on earth and from the deepest, most real part of yourself.

Your love for a mate is fundamental to your nature. That love, that yearning for exquisite, enduring union, throbs beneath your hang-ups, excuses and rational arguments to the contrary.

You want to be totally loved by a mate and to give yourself totally to him or to her.

In spite of your sometimes promiscuous experimentation,

you do not want hit-and-run romance and sex; they are but symptoms of unfulfilled longing.

Perhaps you sense a reservation in yourself – that you aren't so sure you want to give yourself completely to your mate or any mate?

This is another sign of the same loveless disease that is eating the heart out of humanity and crushing the tenderest part of you. You alone are not to blame. For just as you do not love enough, so your mate does not love enough. The result is stalemate.

The awful truth is that man and woman have forgotten how to love sexually. Your bodies remember, but you yourselves do not.

AWAKENING TO LOVE

Sex has become a drug, dulling the loss of love.

HOW TO LOVE, one to another as conscious responsible beings, was forgotten by the human race long ago. And the passage of millennia, rolling from East to West, has compounded the difficulty of remembering, of being awakened to that tragic loss.

If you look closely you will realise you are quite mystified by the sexual act. You know very little about it, even while it's going on, except that it gives pleasure or pain and produces babies.

The real, true purpose of physical love-making has been lost to human consciousness. Sex has become a drug, an opiate of self-forgetfulness for our loveless times – a sort of dream. Consequently your sexual unions are no longer enduring in their own right and are held together mostly by fear, habit and a perverse sense of duty.

Are you being awakened? Are you hearing the truth of what I'm saying?

Let me ask you: What has gone wrong with your love – and nearly everyone else's?

Why are the innocent and youthful expectations of love so predictably and insidiously demolished by the act of physical love?

What do you say has gone wrong?

Isn't it time you took some responsibility for true love on

this planet? Are you going to keep running from the reality, blaming someone or something else? Will you, my beloved man and woman, make a stand with me? Will you, here and now, draw the line between you and lovelessness and say 'Enough!'

Let me tell you in love what the trouble is, and what must be done.

Your worldly experience is the trouble. It has infested you with the fear to love. You are terrified by what you think are the demands of love – when what you are seeing are the demands of your experience, which was not love.

Your mate, due to his or her experience, is just as wary and afraid. And understandably. When you fall in love, and hold back, you miss the point of love and are unhappy. When you give yourself totally you are misused and made wretched. You give a bit of yourself and get a bit of your mate in return; but when you give all, you don't get all. There is no justice in man and woman's love. Nor is there much love in their love. Not as man and woman are now.

The world always wins, always crushes your fondest hopes of love, because you are not yet true to love. As you are, you are lacking in right discrimination. That is, you are unable to tell the difference between love and emotion. You invariably give yourself where there is no love, or only partial love, and it ends in disaster, or stalemate.

You must learn to give yourself totally only to love. Where there is no love, you must not compromise. You must not give in to a biological need without love.

Love must come first – not you or your partner.

LOVE OR SEX?

Make love only for love.

THE GREED OF sex has taken over human lovemaking. You have become insensitive to the fine physical sense of love that you were born with. You have become attached to the emotional demand of sex which seeks satisfaction.

In true love there is no satisfaction, no peace, no rest. Love on earth is a simultaneous union of joy and pain; in its fullness, an ecstatic agony, a cosmic convulsion. To seek only the joy in love, or to feel only the pain, is to reject its rapture and its power. Your emotional greed, or sexual personality, looks for satisfaction in the form of an end, an orgasm – and you are surprised when your loving and lovemaking also come to an end. If you set out to love by looking for a conclusion, a conclusion is what you get.

Unlike emotion and personality, love has no beginning and no end. If you want an orgasm go and masturbate. If you want love then make love without end – by not looking for an orgasm before you start. The man or woman who rediscovers how to love rises above the purely emotional demand of lovemaking. In love, orgasm looks after itself and needs no consideration.

Premature ejaculation, impotence, frustration and frigidity are all due to fear caused by emotional expectation or lack of sufficient love.

Am I making sense?

Never allow a man or woman to hold your hand or embrace you unless you feel the gentle firmness of love in them. Let the greedy grasp of sexual personality go. Even when it appears in a beautiful body it's looking for an end – to get away from you as quickly as possible, once it's gratified.

Be still. Learn to distinguish between the ease of love and the urgent demand of emotion. Love is inexhaustible, irresistible. It is not an urge, not a demand. An urge is a spasm, like the urgent emotional spasm of orgasm. When it is spent, what's left? Nothing, without love.

You must never again let someone love you for that, or like that. You must continue to love physically. But you should endeavour to give yourself only to love, never to a man or woman who is not yet love. If you can hold to this and be love yourself you will gradually raise your mate in love, or draw a more loving man or woman to you.

You will have to be strong. This way of love is not easy.

TRUE LOVE

Where love is, the world is not.

THE INCREDIBLE FACT the world has yet to realise is that the virgin man and woman's innocent fantasies of love, physical and all, are the truth of love. Love is that. Not just like that; love is that – which the world told you was naive. In your innocence you were right all along. Now you have to return to that innocent, simple state of love – in your lovemaking. And the way back is the way of love.

The day you gained your first real experience of physical love the other person involved knew what to do with your body but not what to do with your love. You wanted love and you got sex. You never got over it, and you never will – until you are truly loved. The emotion generated in you that day became the focus of all your previous and subsequent hang-ups.

Sexual ignorance and repression is behind all discontent and unhappiness. Only true love wipes it out. However, let me add this: if you know that on that first day you received love, and love is still personified beside you, then you are divinely blessed and have no need to listen to me.

Man and woman today are for the most part embarrassed or confused when confronted with true love. When I first speak of love there is a feeling of strangeness, of hindrance, of some sort of threat. Sometimes you'd think I was talking about a sexually transmitted disease.

Worldly experience cannot comprehend the love that does not seek to possess any body for itself.

Worldly experience insists on there being an end to everything – whereas love has no end.

You are starved for love because you do not dare to love.

How can your deepest longing – which is to be completely consumed by love – ever be fulfilled if you hide behind the habit of self-protection?

What is it you are protecting anyway?

What have you got to lose by surrendering to love?

All that was originally worthwhile you've already lost – your innocence, your first sweet tender sense of love – because you surrendered it to what was not love. Had it been love, and had you continued to give yourself only to love, you would today be just as innocent, as virginal and enchanted with love, yet with complete sexual awareness.

When I say 'I love you' – and I say it now – you may wonder, 'What does he want from me?'

Such love as mine takes only your confusion, your defences and pretences. If you allow the love, the truth I offer, to enter you, you will start to know again the sense of love you originally knew. And if you can surrender every barrier, every thought, every movement of your mind, to love, you will realise that you are loved forever.

Where love is, the world is not. Where love is, no thorns and thistles grow. When you are truly loved, you are back in Eden.

It is I, love, who speaks to you.

Where I go I leave no footprints, no stain, no residue of world or fear.

I take nothing for myself. I seek only that you be what you

are. And what is that? You are love – as you were in the
beginning and will be in the end that can never be. This you
can realise for yourself by rediscovering how to truly love.

I teach you love by loving you. I weed your gardens and
show you how to prune yourselves. Although the pruning
can be painful, in time you will know you are beginning to
breathe again, even flower again.

But are you man enough to be made man? Are you woman
enough to be made woman? Will you start to take responsibility
for yourself?

YOU ARE RESPONSIBLE FOR LOVE

Cheat on love and you cheat yourself.

How OFTEN DID you talk of love today with the person who shares your life?

Sometimes in the night when you lie together, but are not together, and you turn your face to the wall to bear the emptiness alone, I hear your cry.

Blown roses fill your garden and the thorns and thistles of habit, fear and compromise are choking the life out of you.

Little wonder your despair is sometimes palpable.

You pour your love into your child, pet or job as a substitute for the love of a mate; or because the man or woman in your life will not (cannot) take the pure love and beauty jammed up inside you. And because you cannot take your partner's love, he or she loves outside you.

When you love anything else – even your own child – before rediscovering the love of man or woman, your love is selfish. Your child is on loan to you from another time, another generation which is closed to you and which will leave you behind, in spite of all your loving efforts to keep pace.

Your subconscious, cunning, emotional self knows that in loving other things, which is so easy compared to loving man or woman, its own self-centred existence is not jeopardised. The child, pet, job, or other substitute for human sexual love, cannot accuse you of not loving enough. Only a mate can do that. And it is that we fear and mutually hedge around with the lie of our loveless existence.

Unless each day you speak first of love who do you think you are fooling with your big job, your big name, your independence or aloofness to the pangs and joys of love? Those things are merely self-erected barriers between you and love. They help you to play it safe, while you think you are playing it loose and wild. You only play it loose and wild when you are prepared to lose everything for love.

You are one-eighth married to your partner and seven-eighths married to yourself.

Happily married? Or is it that neither of you can tell the difference between comfort and love?

You live off each other, instead of truly with each other.

You give only what is safe. You give your bodies. And give nothing. You give your emotions, your mind, the years of your lives, and still give nothing.

Did you ever think of giving yourself?

Be honest. If you do not love then say so. And start to love. Face up to it. Try not to blame or justify. Keep the emotion out.

Be straight with each other. In an argument, don't accuse. Ask each other: What's the problem? What are you trying to say? Ask; and listen to the answer. To listen is love.

Remember: you are responsible for your self. This is the first lesson in love.

LOVE WITHOUT FEAR

Be honest to love.

TALK TO YOUR mate of God, truth, love, death and life. All those subjects are in truth one subject – love. Talk from your own spiritual experience, your self-knowledge. By doing that, you declare to each other that love is the most important thing for you.

Only man and woman who can talk of love and truth can discover love together and make love for love instead of making emotion and pain. That is true mating.

It takes two people to make love rightly. If one alone is practising what I teach it will be difficult to make love that does not end in the same old tears, resentment, indifference or depression. Make love for love, and only with a partner who consciously wants to grow in love.

If you do not have a mate, do not turn your back on love. Get yourself right. Prepare yourself by being true and straight.

Do not be afraid. When you are true you will draw right man or woman to you. And when that happens you must declare yourself. Say that you are endeavouring to find God or truth and that your life is directed to this way of love.

It is never too late in life to make love. Do not think you are too old or that it is too late for love to bring a partner to you. Never think you are finished.

Fear can never find love.

Everybody wants to make love. But everybody is afraid. So everybody thinks about it, reads about it, watches movies about it, fantasises about it, jokes about it, lies about it – and is likely to be offended if anyone says 'I want to make love.' And yet it is such a simple and real statement.

The question is: Do you have enough love in you to make love? And do you have enough love in you to be honest?

When you say 'I want to make love' do you communicate love, and not wanting, trying, insensitivity, greed or lust?

Woman's fear of love arises from the dishonesty and loveless-ness of man who only loves when it suits him, who thinks and fantasises about love instead of being love.

Love is first a state of being. Get yourself into the being of love. Then love can provide what you need.

Know that love is not demanding.
Love is giving, not getting.
Love does not hold on.
Love is not offended.
Love is not guilty.
Love is responsible in its actions.
Love does not complain or blame when it is misunderstood.
Love is not afraid.

THE FORGOTTEN SECRET

In perfect sexual love there are three principles:
Man, Woman and God.

MANY MEN WHO do not love are technically brilliant lovers. They have discovered the secret of physical lovemaking; that is, to make love with one purpose – to delight the woman. But superb technique does not unite man and woman in the original divine consciousness. Only perfect lovemaking does that.

By making love rightly man and woman dispel the hurts, disappointments and frustrations that they have accumulated from making love wrongly. Perfect lovemaking dispels all sexual unhappiness.

You men who are anything less than superb lovers have become takers – even though you feel you love your mate. You are impatient to enjoy yourself instead of enjoying the beauty of your partner.

When woman is loved without the haste of self-consideration, she opens out like a flower. And the indescribable spiritual beauty of the female flows to the man.

Love is not a sharing but an exchange.

As much as you men like to think it, your mate is not responsible for your sexual inadequacies. The fault is your own lack of love, which appears as excitement and selfish expectation.

Woman is made for love, for delight, for in those sensations is the truth of herself.

There are no women inexperienced in lovemaking. Each woman comes to puberty perfect in the instinctive ability to make physical love – if she is loved sufficiently.

Love woman with true love and she is a perfect lover every time.

Greedy male sexuality puts fear into woman. Nevertheless, you women are just as irresponsible in love as men, because you have armour-plated yourselves with worldly expectations and misguided concepts of love. Instead of being nothing but love – that is, simply the truth of yourself – you think you know what you want; and how to go about getting it before you start loving. As you lie there, waiting for love, you are still waiting for love and not being love. You must rediscover how to be love – how to be your still, poised self.

Let me show you women just how your misguided, worldly notions of love have subtly become the false, hard part of you. In sexual intercourse you must give up the wretched habit of trying to please your mate. This exploitative obligation, a common neurosis, has been thrust on you by generations of loveless men. When you try to please a man in lovemaking you demean yourself and you lose yourself. You take on the male role – which relieves him of the responsibility of having to learn to love you more.

The truth is: you can only please a man in sexual union, so that he continues to truly love you, when he is able to delight you. Your movements in love are then natural, not acquired contortions. Whether he is pleased or not is up to him and his capacity to love.

In the act of lovemaking you must tell the man if he pleases you and that you love it – why else are you making love with him? – as he must tell you of the beauty and love he finds in you. You must not assume you are communicating what you are feeling or experiencing; you must verbalise it, get it out and help him to love you more. By expressing your joy and love you will also guard against becoming selfish or disappearing into pleasure and self-forgetfulness. You must BE the pleasure – a very conscious participation. Only then is there nothing to say.

You women only draw to yourselves the lovers you deserve. If you have a superb lover it is doubtful that he is faithful. A superb lover can only be faithful to a superb woman.

A superb woman is a woman who loves truth or God. She alone has the power to change man, make him faithful. The woman who loves God most, the most perfect woman, draws to herself the perfect lover – and their union of love never ends.

Now let me tell you another of love's great mysteries – too painful for a loveless world to face up to.

Your utterances of love at any time are real only in that moment. You cannot declare that you will love tomorrow, any more than you can say you will delight in each other tomorrow.

Your love and joy in each other must be made new and fresh every moment, rediscovered day in and day out, and not just in the act of lovemaking. There is no continuity in love; only in our expectation of it. But if you are prepared to love ceaselessly your love is forever.

Union with the Beloved

Beyond all imagining.

Some say the truth I teach is 'masculine'. Fair enough. I am the male principle personified in this body. If this truth is masculine, then there must also be a 'feminine' truth. But how can that be true? —since there is only one truth, one reality, and I am in union with that now.

Union with love is union with all; so at no time is there any distance from the beloved. This love cannot be understood by the human mind; it passes all understanding, all imagining.

Being in union with my love, I can then love man, woman, creature or thing with a love that does not vary and does not end; and my love serves only to affirm the same love in that other being or thing.

As I know my love and am one with her, so I am able to help man and woman discover sensual delight and divine passion in their love of each other.

Is it not the simple task of the male to delight the female, and similarly the female the male? Is it not the heart's desire of the one that the other be made perfect in truth and love? When one is freed from the burden of sexual unhappiness, does that not lead to the delight of both?

In divine lovemaking you discover the rightness and delight of the perfection of pure being. The exchange of energies is what heals division – not just for the couple but in the psyche.

For the being of love is power; a power within space, distance and time, and yet beyond all imagining.

THE WAY OF PRAYER

My prayer –
to be one with the wonder
and beauty of life.

THE FORCE OF PRAYER

What's the use of praying?

WE HUMAN BEINGS have been praying since time began. Whatever we've been praying for doesn't seem to have done much good. Is the world as good as it is, or as bad as it is, because of our prayers? Either way is not much of a recommendation for prayer, is it?

If our prayers ended the last global war, whose prayers started it? And as we prayed for peace then, did we realise that our prayers would help to build the Bomb and end the war in a flash by killing and maiming 300,000 people?

Now we are praying for world peace again. What new calamities are we about to bring down upon the earth?

Do you understand prayer? Do you know the difference between the force of prayer and the power of prayer? I don't think so. For if you did the earth and its people would not be in such an awful mess – poised on the edge of the ultimate in disaster.

Prayer is the most effective, misused and misunderstood force in the world.

Everyone prays. Whether you consider yourself an atheist or materialist is irrelevant. Terms like those are a way of entertaining yourself and have no real meaning. You are a human being. That means you pray. You are praying at this moment, only you don't realise it. It is that unawareness or ignorance that has brought humanity to the verge of annihilation.

You are praying when you are ambitious or working towards an end; when you attempt anything or feel threatened. You pray every moment by hoping – hoping that your plans will work out, that what you are trying to do will succeed, that your next baby will be a boy or a girl, that you won't get sick, that you'll be able to keep a date. You pray every moment by expecting – expecting that what you own will be there when you want it, that your lover still loves you, that death won't trouble you today. You pray when you are being greedy – when you have your eye on the only plate of prawns on the table or the last drink. And when you are impatient, angry or desire sex you are praying very intensely.

To exist and survive in this world is an activity of constant prayer. Rays or waves of vital force radiate out from you into the world as continuous projections of hope – the hope that you will get through and not fail in what you are doing.

The more concentrated and intense you are at any moment, the stronger and more forceful are your personal prayer-waves. Sometimes they reach the pitch of violence.

All this would be harmless if the prayer-waves coming out of us were ineffectual – as we all seem to imagine they are. But they are not ineffectual. They are energetically substantive and accumulative. They have been building up since time began; and today, in their global interaction, they form the world's most destructive, and diabolical, invisible force.

PRAYING FOR SUCCESS

What more do you want?

As PRAYER IS the most effective force in the world, and since everyone continuously seeks and prays to 'not fail', why is there failure in the world?

Failure occurs because success or gain can only come at someone else's expense. For you to be a successful poet, politician or business person (which means that is your constant prayer) some other poor poet, politician or business person has to fail or lose. There is only so much of everything in the world and that includes success or gain.

The success of the world is represented at any moment by what each of its thousands of millions of people have gained. Only so many can be rich because only so many can be poor. The cake of the world, like the energy of the universe, is only so much. There would be ample to go round if everyone were to have only what they need. But because so many have prayed for more than they need, and grabbed it, it's no longer possible for the original losers to get back their share: somebody's already got it. The 'haves', like you and me who can afford the luxury of praying to be successful poets, politicians or business people, are merely playing among ourselves with a share of cake lost by others – while they toil or pray to succeed in not starving. That's why success seems so abstract to us: it's lost the reality of an empty belly.

To the rich of the world we in turn are the poor. The rich, who are few in number but nevertheless have grabbed the most cake or booty, do not struggle or pray to eat – or to be successful poets, politicians or business people. The rich pray only to be successful at keeping the shareout fixed forever as it is. Their prayer is the mightiest in the world. It holds the world together so that all the 'haves' can continue taking and having.

So to succeed in anything, whether as an individual, an organisation or a nation, we have to take from some other person, organisation or nation, somewhere. Which doesn't say a great deal for the way of prayer or way of life that we've devised, does it?

If all our prayers work towards success, how does anyone actually lose? Because some of us are praying for the success of one thing and others are praying for the success of its opposite. One cancels the other out, or the strongest prayer eventually wins. But it can be quite a drawn-out tussle for all but the rich, as living shows. Also, some of us are actually praying for the failure of others and the success of praying for another's failure is of course for them to fail. Then there are half-hearted prayers which get overwhelmed by more intense prayers. And so on.

You'll notice that most of your regular praying, such as that involved in getting you to work each day, succeeds most of the time – as long as it doesn't clash too much with what others want or are praying for. Prayer works – and always for success – otherwise you couldn't make any arrangements at all. You are able to pray pretty confidently by making plans to go on holiday on a certain date, and most times you make it. You can usually manage to keep advance appointments and watch your favourite TV programme. You pray to keep your job and generally do – but if you get lax in your praying or someone starts praying against you, you might lose it.

The whole world of circumstance is the meeting of multiple billions of these prayer-waves – psychic forces – which humanity is continuously giving out. Some harmonise and help each other. Some are inconsonant and opposed. Some attract each other and at the same time are inconsonant – so two cars collide, a company crashes, or a pub full of people gets bombed.

All of this, the uncertainty of living, is the work of the blind force of unconscious, irresponsible, personal prayer.

PIOUS PRAYERS

*Do you really think you know
what's wrong with the world?*

NOW WE COME to the deliberate prayers of all those children (not to mention adults) praying every night and day the world over for someone or other to be blessed or especially favoured; the prayers of you and I, praying for a small miracle when we're in a tight spot, and of billions of others praying indiscriminately all around the earth to right the world's apparent ills.

At this point I have to ask you a question, very seriously: Did you really think that all those innocent-sounding prayers could be projected continuously into the world by generation after generation without setting in motion some sort of law of cause and effect? Did you perhaps even venture to assume that if nothing else, they were harmless?

If such prayers are not effective, why does humanity pray? Why has it always prayed? And if its prayers are effective, who said they are only effective of good? Have you ever thought about this?

Here's another very serious question: Do you really think you know what's wrong with the world? —sufficient to take it upon yourself to pray to try to change it for what you think would be better?

And do you trust the judgment of all those others, including the children, who are also praying because they think they know what's wrong, or what would be better?

Are you prepared to be answerable, in your own life, for all the changes involved in making the one change you pray for? Would you pray so easily, and sleep so untroubled, if you knew that the effect of all your prayers – not just the one you're praying for – comes back on you? For that is precisely what happens.

Remember, all the prayers of the human race, unconscious and deliberate, are knitted up together and this has been going on since time began – prayer-waves contending with each other to work themselves out as circumstances in the world and continuing to do so ages after the generations who prayed them are forgotten. The result is that a stupendous ferment of unexhausted prayers, a mighty field of force, has built up around the simplicity of the earth and its people. This field of force is the world. The combined effect of all the praying descends continuously on humanity. That effect is the condition of the world at any moment – the circumstances in which you and I and the rest of the earth's people must endeavour to live our little lives.

FLASHPOINT

Time's almost up.

WHAT THE WORLD is facing today, with justified trepidation and a deepening sense of disaster, which will turn to terror, is a mighty moving mountain of undischarged responsibility for all our blind, selfish and irresponsible praying. The force that went out of us and made the world what it is, has returned to claim its source. It is here and it's about to come down on us.

The force of the world has reached flash-point – the brink of disaster, not for just a few nations, as in 1945, but for all nations. You don't have to believe me. Keep checking the daily news media and listen to the growing public protests of the worried people of the earth. There is no escape. It's heads down for all of us.

Much of what I am now going to say will be unsettling and disturbing. It will linger in you. To the extent that you are real it will keep coming up in your awareness and cause a lot of self-searching.

In what follows I am making a positive statement about life now, and the future of life on earth, but in the present depressed condition of humanity it is likely to be perceived as negative.

The world as we know it is finished. There is going to be an awful wipe-out. Just about all the earth's population will be destroyed. But not quite all. The human race will survive.

The end can come any day. No day is safe any more. Our

constant prayer for favouritism and peace-from-war, instead of justice for all, has produced the means of global destruction and ever since its invention the margin of time has been closing. Now, apart from the daily period of waiting, time's up. All that can be done in the world has been done. Whatever is done now is just another move in the step towards the end. Things can't get better except in the imagination and the daily media. All the peace movements, all the prime ministers, presidents and armies – even the loftiest, most selfless actions – can't prevent what's coming.

Do you want to argue that what I'm saying isn't true? Do you want to stop reading, and try to push the whole thing out of your mind? Or go merrily on your complacent way, imagining it's okay – someone or something will work it out and save the day?

This is not a bad dream that you're going to wake up from. It's reality. Please look at it.

Many people will be dismayed by what I am saying. That is unavoidable. But I want to help you to see and understand what is going on, for it is because you have not faced up, not understood the world, that you are now frightened or apprehensive. I didn't invent the peril; you don't get dismayed or frightened by fiction. It's the authenticity of the situation, presented without any fantasy of escape, that will dawn on you – penetrate you.

As a spiritual teacher it is my responsibility to reveal to you the truth. I am telling you the truth of the world and what's going to happen – and it may happen any day now.

When you look closely at what I'm saying you'll see it is not so different from what the more reflective people of the earth have been saying for some decades: if you don't desist you're going to blow us all up. Well, we haven't desisted and I'm telling you it's now too late for the 'if' – the hope.

No Hope

Where is there anything of lasting value?

WE LIVE ON hope in this world. We have to live in hope. I am removing your hope. But did you really have any? Of course not. There's no hope in this world because you're going to die.

Like the world, you can die any day. But you keep yourself from going mad with the thought of this by living in hope, in the fantasy that you'll die some distant tomorrow. The fact that the world is now about to die too is really incidental. It's terrifying because it means you've run out of tomorrows, run out of world to escape into.

How can you go on in the world if it's going to end? —You go on exactly as you are. Nothing's changed. How did you go on each day before, when you knew you were going to die?

I am not going to give you hope. But I am going to give you more of the truth which is the strength of life.

I have said that the world is going to be destroyed, not the earth. That is very important to remember; because it is the earth, not the world, that you love. The earth will be here; and if you come to life in the time you've got, you'll be here too.

The earth and the life-forms on it will receive a savage, punishing blow. The earth too has to pay a penalty, as it's already doing, for the selfishness of the intelligent life – us – that came out of it. We humans are of the earth; we are the life-forms of intelligence on earth; and out of us came the human intelligence that created the world.

The earth is responsible for us as a mother is responsible for her child. If the child is irresponsible or unloving, the mother must suffer in some way.

Our tremendous free-wheeling intelligence is the problem. We are very clever, very smart children. But right from the beginning we have been takers. With our unfeeling intelligence and selfish greed we took from the mother without consideration until a third of her was reduced to desert, for which we cleverly blamed the elements; and at the same time we took from each other until half of us were starving or impoverished, for which we again cleverly blamed everything but ourselves. Without let-up the mother and the life on the earth continue to be denuded and deprived by our rapacious intelligence. At every level of existence human intelligence has demonstrated greed and exploitation using the excuse and euphemism of progress.

Progress is essential, says human intelligence. Is it? Or is it only essential when you're running from something?

The trouble is: we got it wrong to start with. Our intelligence should have been the servant; that is, it should have served some real value. But the human race has had no real values – nothing of worth that ever lasted. And with nothing to serve but its shifting self-interest, the smart servant became the clever master.

Today we still serve nothing of value – only progress and convenience. What do you serve, give your life to, that is not your own? What is the world devoted to?

We simply don't know what to do with our intelligence. We're stuck. We're going towards self-destruction and we can't stop.

Keep reading the newspapers: it's actually happening. All we can do is fight and oppose, be for or against, vote this way or that, and hope for a final compromise. That's all human intelligence knows.

Will you try a different way? Put your intelligence second? Will you give life itself a chance?

LIFE GOES ON

Our achievements destroy us.

IS THERE ANYTHING human intelligence has created that is worth saving in this world? What in the world is worth preserving?

Would you make a mental list please?

Persons? If you think certain persons are worth saving, then why does everybody die? —and many of them very young. Life on earth, which is still the master of death, doesn't rate persons as valuable at all; though our intelligence tries to. Life is indeed valuable. That's why it's always here. But persons come and go; as you and I will.

The person you are is not the being you are. The being is what I endeavour to address. The person is what you and I project into the world and give a name to. My person is called Barry Long. The person you are is what performs and reacts in the world. The person – every person who ever lived – is what has brought us to this awful point.

Art? Our intelligence has murdered art. The art we think of as art is a last pitiful remnant of the great art that once was life on earth itself; the great art of being a human being – before the intelligent person took over.

Why do so few of the earth's population value what we call 'art', even in our own intelligent society? Why is there so much room in art for posturing and humbug? The answer is: It is not art. It's just all we've got left, all we can muster at the end of an inglorious intelligent era. A few paintings, statues, texts, buildings – all we've got to show for five thousand years of intelligent civilisation, of creeping westernisation.

What makes the priceless treasures in art galleries and museums so valuable? —The price that intelligence long ago put on them. And what of our arts today – our dance, music, film, painting, sculpture, words? Are they memorable? Are they alive? Or just getting a living for those who try so hard to give them life? Are they truly worth preserving? Do they have the worth of the creative spirit itself? Or have we debased the creative living spirit that was Man – ourselves, the great art on earth? Have we replaced it with our human intelligence, which is no more the living spirit than its fruitless offspring, the sterile spaceship, computer and nuclear reactor?

What about ideas? —such as those that developed the means of creating electricity, space travel and our high-tech, high-convenience society. Perhaps you think they're worth saving? That's because you can't see life beyond progress, beyond the Bomb.

Our ideas do not serve anything of real value; they all go in one direction – away from life, or the earth, towards death, the nuclear bomb or the cultured germ. We can't get rid of the bomb, or its cultured partner, no matter how hard we try, because our technology will invent a better device – a simpler, easier one; a do-it-yourself more instant one. It can't be avoided. That's the way we think. That's progress.

Hoping to improve the world we develop wonderful ideas; and invariably they contribute to greater competition, rivalry, political opportunism, fear, and exploitation of space, nature and people – because we don't know what to serve. Our intelligence is out of control. The rich have won. The share-out stays fixed. In winning at the expense of others we have lost it all.

Anything that is worth preserving is of the earth and not of our civilisation. Our achievements are completely expendable, as were those of all previous civilisations. Nothing of any consequence has survived any of them – except the earth and the life on it, which is all that will survive of this civilisation.

Your dismay and attempt to disbelieve what I am saying is because you happen to be at the end of this civilisation. Life is the same at the end of every civilisation. And of course it's almost impossible for you – as it was for all the others at the end of their civilisations – to imagine that your world is finished. Would you please look at this. See whether it is true. For I can only point out the truth. You have to perceive it for yourself.

All previous civilisations were corrupt like ours – futile attempts by man to create a world of his own on the already perfect earth. They all destroyed themselves eventually, or unsuspectingly allowed themselves to be destroyed, through what they considered to be their finest achievement. In our case the means of destruction will be our scientific genius, our intellectual materialism.

THE END OF THE WORLD

It takes tragedy to change us.

MAN IS TO undergo an enormous change in consciousness as a result of the catastrophic tragedy he will witness and be totally involved in. The experience will disintegrate all the old patterns of his mind, incendiarise and purge the human psyche to its foundations and transform self-consciousness on earth.

No class of person will be left out. No politicians, industrialists, royalty, financiers, generals, scientists or workers will be left to imagine and discuss the carnage from protected positions. Every individual will be the battlefield of personal soul-raking tragedy.

Why? Why in the purpose of things is such horrific devastation and suffering necessary? —Because only personal tragedy changes man. Of all the tragedy that there has ever been in the world, it has never affected the majority before. Consequently, man who lives off the imagined security of the majority – the world – has changed very little. This time, however, engulfed in total tragedy of his own making which leaves no escape, no room for discussion or fantasy, man will change. It will literally blow the world out of him.

From our worldly point of view man will know enormous personal suffering for a long time. But he will not see it that way. He will not recover and embrace the world again, as we do now when tragedy strikes here and there. He will never be that man again. He will be a creature of higher consciousness.

It is impossible for the human mind to imagine what the new life on earth is to be. We cannot conceive of the earth without the world. All our imaginings are of the world, of our self-consciousness, and are not true. But by simply listening to what I have to say, and not employing your worldly faculties of thinking back or reasoning, you will hear the truth; and you may notice a subtle excitation in your being. It is the world alone that prevents you from hearing the truth or being what you really are.

As the world within and without him vanishes, man will come in contact with the powers I am endeavouring to reveal in you now. These powers, guiding man from within, will be intensely real and discernible, because they will no longer have to come through the deadening barrier of the world. Helped and directed by these powers, man will be intelligent and responsible – since at last he will have found something of enduring value. He will have discovered the reality of life on earth. And self will have been obliterated from his self-consciousness.

Everything worth preserving is in man and the rest of the species and will continue after the end of the world. The men and women who survive will love, serve and know life – as man and woman have longed to do, but have not been able to do for thousands of years. The survivors will be in continuous intimate contact with life within them as living spirit, and with the earth and life around them as one living organism. They will have an enlightened aversion for the past and retain practically no memory of it. They will not long for what has been. They will know that it was the past – that

122

which we defended as our way of life and allowed to happen – that decimated the earth and the life on it. They will have no sympathy at all for the likes of us, no affection for us. They will regard us as the unforgivable barbarians who wantonly and wilfully deflowered the earth. And if people like us reappear, the world will be summarily obliterated from them, just as it had been from the earth and the survivors.

The men and women who survive will have nothing to learn, nothing to study and distract them; nothing that would allow another world like ours to build up again. They will have learned the only lesson to be learned from living, which we never learned; that to lose contact with the powers within by trying to create another world with human intelligence is inevitable disaster.

Man as the conscious surviving part of future life on earth will retain his creative genius, but it will be controlled by the creative spirit within him. He will no longer have anything to do with progress. He will have discovered a real value to serve, the value of life. And his ideas will work for life, for good; not for death or gain.

ALL TO THE GOOD

We have to bring life back to earth.

HAVEN'T YOU FELT for most of your life that your views and opinions should be respected; that even in some small way you're entitled to have a say or a hand in determining your destiny – by voting, by making decisions – or that you should at least be considered or consulted? Well, you're right. The final responsibility is yours. It is your world after all.

Incredible, isn't it? —that it should all finally depend, or descend, on you.

Everyone of us feels that we're somehow important; that our life must have some purpose beyond just living and dying. Many have been inspired by the idea or example of Jesus dying for the world. Dare you put yourself on the same level?

Dare you not?

In the time we've got, let's get it right, or more right, for the time after. I am not asking you to join a peace movement, to believe in anything or make any kind of protest or public announcement. I'm just asking you to take responsibility for being a human being on this earth.

You may think you're already taking this responsibility. But what you've been taking responsibility for is the person you are, not the being you are; and no overt action by any person or persons can change what's coming – the world's confrontation with its own reality, the truth of its own making.

The only change that can be effective for good has to happen in you, the individual being. In the time that is left you have to change your person, transform it, metamorphose like the butterfly. You can do this only by making and continuing to make the ultimate personal sacrifice; which is to willingly surrender the person you are on behalf of the greater good, the human race. Only by you doing this can man make a fresh start on earth.

Humanity of the future has to have new resources of spirit to draw on – which only you, the individual, can provide. You have to be, not a martyr in the physical sense, but a super-person in the real sense. And you've got to do it alone. No one else is going to listen or hear – only you.

You can't leave it to fate because fate's against you. It's fate, Nemesis itself, that's coming.

You can't even leave it to God, Jesus, the Buddha or any other divinity. God, Jesus, the Buddha, the spirit of mankind, can and definitely will save you, the being. There's no doubt about that: you are already saved, because there is no death. But God can't save the world of persons from its fate, or the world from itself.

Yet you can give the new earth a new kind of person. The question is: Will you?

We are the only threat to the future of the human race. The future life on earth has got to be saved from us – from our ingrained irresponsible way of thinking and our selfishness. Selfish means we can't help but project our selves into every thing we do. We know of no alternative because we don't know what is good.

What is good? I ask you now . . .

What is good? —as if you don't know.

We all know: life is good.

Life on earth is good; or it was until the human race selfishly created another sort of life – living in the world. As the world spread over the earth, life, the good, diminished; and living, convenience, got easier. So today living is relatively easy with its scientific gadgetry and enlightened dole queues; but life – the inner enriching, revivifying 'good' – is that much harder to find. And any day now, as the world finally demonstrates its crowning achievement in gadgetry or living, there won't be much life around at all.

But life is still good, isn't it? It is still good beneath the strangulation of the world that we all experience. To get back down to life, all we have to do is rid ourselves of the world. But as that can't be done without destroying it, as the pressure and force of living is about to do, the only alternative is to rid the world of ourselves. That means getting rid of the rubbish, shedding the worldly person to reveal the being underneath.

You and I have to start now, today, voluntarily eliminating our problematical personal self from within – before circumstances do it from outside. Otherwise the new life on earth will be a carbon copy of living in the old world. And the force will quickly build up again to destroy that world too.

The immediate task is to free this planet and its people, as much as can be accomplished in the time we've got, from the cumulative effects of our misguided prayers and personal prayer-waves. What we pray for is what we get. That is our fate, and in a world of persons where everyone is praying for something different, the fate is eventual disaster. We must not go on adding to the mass of that incurably selfish personal praying. And we have to be sure that our prayers today don't bring down misfortune tomorrow. In other words, you and I have to reverse the work of the force of prayer through the power of right prayer.

126

RIGHT PRAYER

The power of prayer brings us back to life.

THE WAY OF prayer I am going to present to you is a way to
help save the earth and its people of the future. By helping you
to understand prayer and the reality behind what's happening
in the world, I am putting you in touch with new powers
within your being, powers deep in the unconscious, that are
now rising and ready to be released for good.

To pray rightly you must not pray for anything to happen
or not happen in the world.

You must stop your children and yourself from asking for
blessings for others. You must not pray by asking for the sick
or troubled to be made well or untroubled. You must not ask
to reverse the condition of anyone; or pray for anyone to
receive anything. Praying for people like that only transfers
misfortune from one place to another.

When your prayers work to help a person (and they often
do, because all prayer works towards success) you are taking
something from someone else in the world somewhere.
That person's condition will worsen; and it might be yourself, for your prayers come back on you, remember. It's not
uncommon for someone close to a sick person to also
become ill, after the person has recovered or died. Multiply
this effect by a billion prayers a day and you get the poverty,
misery and suffering that never leaves this world.

Praying for people releases force. What the afflicted in this

127

world need is not more force, but more power – more life and love. Power is all positive; whereas force is positive and negative, and thus creates the world of opposites, of pain and gain. When you pray for a particular person to be saved, you leave someone else out. So you upset the balance of life and create the condition of injustice in living that requires someone to lose for another to gain. You make the world stronger and you contribute to the unhappiness of life on earth. It must be that everyone is blessed; not just someone whom you think should be.

To pray rightly you must resist the urge to pray for particular people to be saved. Instead, simply hold the image of them, or their energy, within you. As you hold the image, love them. Unite with their energy within you. Keep the corners of your mouth up. Smile a little. Don't allow yourself to think about the past, your sadness or loneliness; and don't cry. Stay with their energy within you.

By resisting the urge to pray for them, by not using force which is the way of the world, power (or life and love) is released within you. And because you are holding the energy of the person (rightly containing your concern for them) the power will go to them. They will be comforted in some way even though their external circumstances may not appear to change; for all things must die as some things must fail. But you will have released the power of good into existence.

The power of prayer, unlike the force of prayer, will not deprive another to heal or comfort the one you are concerned for. The power will go wherever it is needed in the world without having any injurious, negative effect.

And don't try to pray for 'everyone'.

You and I are not large enough, just and wise enough, loving, humble and selfless enough, to pray for the earth and all its people. To take responsibility for such a prayer you would have to be life itself, the power itself. And then there would be no need for the prayer, or the pray-er.

Do you see this? With our self-projecting, self-selected prayers we wrap the goodness of the earth, and those who come and go on it, in a short-sighted, unjust world.

Nevertheless you must pray. But pray as often as you can without an image in your mind.

Pray for yourself. Pray to be one with life, one with the good, one with the earth, one with the source, one with God.

Find the life within you. Don't think about it: sense it. You're alive, aren't you? —so life must be there. Find it. Sense it. Be it.

Stop giving yourself to the world. Give yourself to life. Sink into the sensation of it. Give yourself to the good within you.

Then the power will work in you and through you. You will find you are truly serving people in the world. And you will know that you are coming to life.

The power is with you – if you give up the force.

129

PRAYERS OF FREEDOM

I pray that the world may be free of my self.

THE ERROR OF the world is in you and me. Free the world of your error and you free it of yourself. Free it of yourself and you create a little bit of space for love and rightness to surface in the world and work for good.

To free the world or anything of yourself is to help to heal it. Love and rightness are there ready to work on any condition of sickness, poverty or misery – once you create the necessary space in your being by getting yourself out of the way.

Pray for the starving and suffering of the world like this:

'I free you of my anger, my greed and my thoughtlessness; and of my thoughtfulness in wanting to change things for you without giving my life to you or for you.

'I free you of my opinions about what caused your condition. I free you of my interest in reading about and viewing your misery, in seeing your emaciated bodies and hearing about your suffering, while my own belly is full.'

The people whose bellies we feed today will be hungry again tomorrow. Or if they're not, some other people will be. All are suffering from the same disease, the same condition of the world – the lack of life and love in you and me.

'I free you of my ignorance in thinking that I was really sorry for you, or that I really helped you when I sent you money and food. For that money and food, which I didn't

130

need, must have come from someone else – from yourself, perhaps, or from those who must starve tomorrow. How did I come to have so much when you have nothing? You weren't always hungry. Who took it from you and gave it to me?

'All the prayers of the privileged certainly worked against you, didn't they? Made us rich and you hungry. Your prayers must have been too simple, too natural, and you lost out. Now it looks as if we've been too smart and prayed ourselves into a far greater impoverishment than yours.

'I know now that I must help to end the condition that causes your poverty and hunger. I must give up my self, give up my selfish prayers and this foolish, thoughtless, thinking person who thought that misery was natural on the earth.'

Pray to free the world of your personal self.

'I free the world of my prayers. I pray for nothing in the world. I want nothing from the world except what I am given and what I earn.

'I free the world of my concepts of what is good and of what should be changed.

'I free you – everyone and everything – from any emotional demands I have put on you. I let the emotion in me go, knowing that love never leaves; that finally all persons and things depart, but never my love.'

The strength of life is its power to keep giving – giving of itself, not holding on to anything.

What have I got to give? Only what I would hold.

'I hold on to nothing that anyone has said or done in the past.

'I free you from inside me, where I've been holding you a prisoner in my own dim, fearing world. If you come back and try to make me hold on to you with my resentment, envy or wanting, I pray that I might have the strength of life to let you go again in love.'

Pray to be free of the pressure of the world.

'I have no quarrel with the world. I know it is cruel, violent and difficult. But at least I know where I stand and so I will not be surprised by what the world does to me.

'I live, work and perform in the world. But I do not love the world. I love life and the earth. And in that I am immortal.'

Don't try to exclude the world from your life for that will only create resistance and add more pressure. You live in this world. You helped to make it. You just can't disown it or get out of it. Do what you must in the world, but don't be confused by it. Give it its due, but not more. Don't be deceived by it. And don't add to it by trying to change it. Change yourself instead.

Transform yourself by being more loving, more patient and aware. Die to your self daily for the power. Help others who are receptive, and especially your children, to understand the difference between life and the world, power and force. See yourself as responsible for life and the earth every moment – not only when you feel like it or have the time. Don't hurt life or the earth any more than you have to. Yet don't feel guilty for what you may have done. Make a fresh start now. The earth forgives our transgressions.

Be of good cheer. Life is now.

A PRAYER FOR LIFE

I pray to be one with life and love.

'I LOVE. I LOVE life. I love being alive.

'Because I love life, I love many things, or at least some things; but there are things I do not love and do not even think about. As all things are in life, and that life is in me now, I pray that I may love life more, that I may know it more within me, and in this way reach all things that may need more life and love.'

Teach your children to pray with their being; and not with their thoughts.

Pray at all times; in the bus or the train, or while you are walking.

Pray while you are making love.

Pray and allow the life, the wonder, to swell in you.

Don't be concentrated. Smile a little. Be open. Be empty.

Be loving. Be giving.

Pour out your being, without thought or intention, as the bird pours out its being in song.

Above all, live the prayer.

133

THE PATH AND THE WAY

All paths lead to frustration, doubt, impatience, fear;
so take the path of least ignorance
– until you find the way, the one way,
which is your whole life.

No longer attached to living for a result
I am on the way, the only way,
– my life as it is now.

WHAT AM I DOING?

I don't understand.

IN THE SPIRITUAL life confusion is better than certainty. It symptomises the breaking-up of the understanding and the experiential ground of the brain. The certainty of the brain ignorantly convinces humans that they are not going to die. This is most evident in youth, whereas in the elderly it's normal for holes or fragmentation to show up in the understanding. In them the understanding breaks up because it's served its purpose and soon will die with the body. When humans at any age suddenly face death, which cannot be understood, they are helpless, confused and likely to go to pieces.

In the spiritual life the 'holes' in the understanding are made by consciousness. Consciousness does not die.

'But I'm still looking for answers', you say, 'I really don't know what the hell I'm doing or who I am.'

And I say: Do not try to understand or work out what I, the master, am saying. Just read and re-read my words. Listen while I show you how to be. Give up trying. When the time comes, you will know what to do, simply by doing.

The ceaseless demand of the brain is for instant, quick-fix answers. But answers beget puzzles, and more answers, and more puzzles. Only the master can give the real answer, which is the solution.

The puzzle of existence is merely an invention to fill the vacuum of 'no-answer' in the brain. The puzzle forms and becomes the search for 'reality'. But the search eventually leads back to the spiritual vacuum, where there is no thinking, no questioning and no understanding.

When westernised man and woman reach the vacuum in the brain they think they are going mad when in fact they are going sane. In reality they are going East – East of the brain which long ago went West.

The East is the master, the living truth in man and woman. The West is the know-all that rubbishes it. East and West are poles apart in the human psyche. The East ends and the West begins in you – in your discontent and avoidance of the truth. God, like life and truth, is East of questions, of ignorance, of knowing and not-knowing – East of Eden.

Now you must cross from West to East, which is to go back through yourself into the reality of being. Going back East there is suffering. The order of suffering is from the horrible, to the terrible, to the awful. To the westernised brain this is appalling, an ever-increasing pressure of suffering. But seen from the East, it is the reverse: a diminishing. What is awful is the moment of truth, the moment of God; for God alone is awe-ful. In the West man and woman run from the awful truth; yet facing it is the only solution to what is horrible and terrible – the never-ending discontent and the lack of fulfilment of every westernised man and woman.

Cross the brain-made desert you must. There is no other way. It is your way, because you made it when you went West. Now you must retrace your steps, leaving behind all you have gathered, all your attachments. All you will retain for the journey is your love and your experience. Everything else is useless baggage and will only hamper you on the extraordinary crossing.

Know that it all happens in you. No one but the master can help you. No one will understand. Nothing is achieved, but everything is accomplished.

You cannot set out before you are ready. You cannot board the boat at the end of the pier until the pier is built. Lack of preparation for the truth is all that restricts you; and all that protects you from the awful consequences.

The Path Is Not The Way

The way is out of time.

THE ONLY METHOD of self-realisation is living itself. Everyone is born on that same path. But the path is not the way.

Living is the workshop of unconscious growth and development, the spasmodic evolution of the mass of humanity through time-waves of disaster, war, poverty, fire and flood; through disease, fading values, hardening attitudes, drastic change, birth and death. The blindly striving human mass is always there, with nothing to live for apart from living, nothing to die for, and everything to leave. Living like that is the path of circumstance by which the individual reaches the way.

An individual reaches the way when he or she comes through this unconscious process of living to the point of consciously seeking the truth. There is the awareness of wanting something different, and not knowing what; of longing and yearning for a kind of release.

The individual starts to look for something outside time. But what can be beyond the grip of time? This self-pondering is the beginning of the way. Rejecting the continuity of unconscious living and dying, the individual starts to long for the realisation of living. In other words there is a longing for life, the timeless, the immortal.

On the path of living only experience points the way. There are no spiritual teachers on that path. But at the beginning of the way, the teacher becomes essential; and then manifests.

The realisation of life, immortality, what I am, or any of the other extreme points in consciousness is direct. These are not concepts, precepts or percepts; they are eternally present ideas, 'there' in the individual's consciousness to be realised as quickly as possible through direct experience. An individual on the way to realisation has to become more and more sensitive to the extraordinary energy of direct experience – experience not dependent on the senses, the emotions, the memory or the imagination. In fact, the way is the process of being made sensitive to it.

Living is indirect experience. No energy or knowledge arrives straight; it all comes through the senses and there is always 'this-or-that'. Any realisation depends on the ability to separate the indirect experience of a condition from the direct experience of a state. A condition changes; a state does not. A state is self-sufficient, a unity. For instance, the state of life and the condition of living are two distinctly different, superimposed energies, but the normal mind is too disordered and diffused to distinguish the truth, or to hold the experience of living separate from the state of life in consciousness. To do this requires the power of distinction, or the ability to realise 'this is not that', and the power to hold the realisation so that the unity of being is known at any moment.

Although everyone alive is on the same path to conscious realisation – truth cannot be exclusive – we are all at different levels of development and evolutionary awareness. But as well as our limitation this is our protection. We can only advance in consciousness at the pace we have inured ourselves to withstand.

141

The highest realised consciousness needs nothing, wants nothing; and living is neither necessary or unnecessary. To realise this before the psyche is self-sufficient, to suddenly participate in the appalling aloneness of this state, its forever-ness and terrifying nothingness, would be diabolical – literally hell. So the whole scheme of things (and this is evidence of its sublime integrity) is a graduated process of evolutionary preparation – the extraordinary phenomenon called life.

LIFE, THE TEACHER

There is always a teaching.

ESOTERICALLY IT CAN be said that life consists only of
teaching and learning, which is mostly done unconsciously;
and that everyone, not just the 'advanced' or religiously aware,
is provided with a teacher or teaching at every stage of life
from birth to death. In other words, the teacher is life itself.

How does this all-pervading teaching work and manifest as
circumstances? Esoterically, every living thing draws to itself the
essential requirements for its own physical survival and growth.
For instance, plant-life attracts water and although water may
be withheld by drought or circumstance from individual
plants, plant-life as a whole survives and flourishes for the
simple reason that it rains. Plant-life and water each attract and
support the existence of the other. So it is with the spirit. The
degree of a person's conscious development determines the
kind of teaching 'sustenance' that he or she needs and attracts.

Everyone's spiritual or conscious need manifests as individual
interests and enthusiasms. We follow our interests and
engage in them. When we meet people who can give us a
new slant on our pet subjects we call it 'interesting', and they
in turn refer to us when we are in a position to help or
encourage them. We derive immense satisfaction out of
receiving and giving in this way. Every day at the ordinary
level of conversation with friends, family, workmates and
even strangers, we are continuously exchanging information
and swapping roles as teacher and student.

We can really only help or listen when we are interested. So our interests propel us towards those who need us, and those whom we need. We are all learning. We are all teaching. Everyone in his or her own way is a guru.

What is the truth of interest and enthusiasm?

Every individual interest is a desire, first to absorb and digest a subject; and second, to radiate that knowledge out to others, enriched by our own particular understanding and experience of the matter. We discuss and share our interests. Again, we alternate ceaselessly as the teacher and the taught.

So what is the necessity for spiritual teachers or the spiritual master?

As you will have noticed by now, an interest in the truth is not enough. Interest or enthusiasm for the truth may bring you to self-enquiry, but does not bring self-knowledge. Endless late-night discussions about God, truth or the universe produce only opinions, more and more avenues to explore, more and more paths away from the simple, intimate truth that can never be expressed like that. Only one who has no interest in the world, who is detached from it, can show you the way.

It is the way of life that when you become more interested in truth than the world you are drawn to the teacher or teaching you need. Then life's unconscious teaching becomes the conscious spiritual life.

How does it happen that the teacher comes when you are ready?

Whatever degree of self-knowledge you possess, that is your centre of gravity – the pulling-power of your particular level of consciousness. It radiates and emits abstract waves of a particular positive value. These attract a corresponding and polarising force in the form of the teacher or teaching that you need.

For Love or Money

Nothing is free.

THE TRUTH IS yours naturally. You already have it. It cannot be acquired, given or taken. It is therefore not natural to teach the truth. However you need a teaching to rid yourself of what is unnatural in you – your unhappiness, pain and anguish. When that is done you no longer need the teaching, which is your last unnatural need.

Love is the currency of truth as money is the currency of the world. Everything that is unnatural in the world needs money for its survival. I teach you to die to the world while you survive in it. My teaching keeps you alive, not with money but with love. It is for you to receive that love, to be with it, and finally to be it – so that love and not money is in control of your worldly circumstances.

This love is not the love you know, which you can define, or know as 'mine'. That love is personal and will one day cause you pain. The cleansing spirit of truth will sweep through it, but since it must come through possessive or exclusive love its teaching is indirect or limited; and limitation is always painful. The love you think you know, represented by a person, object, idea or notion of yourself, continually vanishes and turns to pain. You have so often been happy. And what happened? If you are happy now, please observe how long it lasts. The truth is any love or happiness you can name is doomed. It is doomed by the world in you, the unnatural.

145

I am here to show you another love, to help you overcome the world in you, to find yourself, to find real love and then to be it.

The teaching of truth does not come free. If you want it you must pay. You pay in money. Or you pay in love and service. Or you pay in pain and confusion. Take your pick.

I am here to take you out of the world, but you must pay your way. You must not leave it to others to pay for you. Pay gladly and the love you cannot know or name will look after you.

Those that are closest to the master pay in pain – until they discover sufficient love of God to go on paying in love and service every moment.

To be with the truth in this world is a privilege. We must pay for our privileges.

But let's be practical. It takes money for the truth I am to be available through my presence, through books, teachings on tape and so on. Who pays for it all? You do – through your payment of money.

In order to receive the truth, you must give. And you contribute not just for yourself but so that others may have what you have received. Everything is poured back.

I teach that no one is special. Or everyone is special.

Many persons and groups of people in this world ask to be treated as special. They want a concession. But if the truth, wherever you seek it, is not above every consideration in your life it is not the truth you are seeking.

Whenever you say that you can't pay or can't do what the ordinary man and woman seeking the truth have to pay or do, you make yourself special. That is an extraordinarily responsible action for you to take. Where the truth of yourself

146

is concerned, by declaring yourself a special case you immediately invoke the law of life; which means you ask to be judged whether or not you are being true. The door will be open to you to receive the truth; but then, to the degree that you are being true, your circumstances will change either for better or for worse.

You alone are responsible for the condition of your life – not the government, not some condition or misfortune. Your world is what you are. There is no one to blame for it. You are the only limitation and problem in your life.

To change your world you must change yourself. You do it by learning to free yourself every moment of the world within you – the unnatural. As you do that you free yourself of the limitations of the world around you. You come back to life.

But you cannot do it on your own. And you cannot receive love as the currency of truth without giving in the currency of the world.

A WAY OF UNLEARNING

The world is what you have learned.

WHATEVER IS OF real value – once you find it – you live; and you can only live it now. You can't shut it up in a museum or a book; and you can't study it or learn it.

You can't study life on earth. You are life on earth, so you can't learn it; you can only love it and be it. The only things you can study are life-forms, or formulas. And life-forms are not life.

There are no scholars, professionals or professors of life; nor of love, which is the true value of life on earth. All scholars and practising students study the world and are of the world. They are all as lacking in life and love – that is, as dead – as the things they study.

In precisely the same way, all the world's workers, and all its wealthy players, who have lost touch with life and love are as dead as the world they toil and play in.

Learning and studying are not natural processes. That's why even when we love a subject we often find the necessary learning tedious.

To be successful at anything we have to do a lot of studying, learning and practising. Everything in the world has to be learned. Even arts of self-expression, such as singing, painting, dancing, writing, making music, must be studied and practised. Why does it require such effort? Why must we sacrifice so much of our time and energy to study and practice? It's because the great effort of learning, and the years required to master anything, including school subjects, are the action of breaking through the awful crust of the world that encases each one of us. It's a way of penetrating to the natural being underneath.

How much of your life have you spent learning? Are you still learning now – struggling to break through the world in some way or other? It's due to that exhausting effort that you seldom feel really alive. You have had to surrender great slices of your beautiful life on earth and give them to the world. But after enough precious life has been sacrificed to the monster, after the sweat and tears of learning, how easy, joyful and fulfilling it is to express ourselves. You've noticed this, haven't you?

Learning is completely unnecessary – but only after the world has been removed from the person. While the world is there – and it's in everybody on earth – you have to go on learning and sacrificing your life for it.

We don't get much time for enjoying our life on earth any more. Every day the world requires man to make a greater sacrifice of his time or life.

To be successful, young people must study hard and work harder and harder. Some give up and drop out; but since this world is everybody's rat race, no one is excused the required sacrifice, for it must be made one way or another – if not in time, then in pain, boredom or tears. So many teenagers don't know what they want to do with their lives. That's the world in them, a deadening weight on the natural bent for self-expression. Yet each individual is born with a natural ability to contribute something uniquely worthwhile to life and the earth – if only it can be reached through the learning of the world.

Even if you give the world your entire life – which most people are doing today – it still won't deliver the goods. The world always short-changes you. To be an accomplished or successful dancer, painter, actor, computer programmer, financier, or anything else, only means that after all the years of effort you've only broken through to yourself in that one tiny area. The rest of your existence in this world remains as difficult as anyone else's. Even the world's most successful and powerful people worry, feel cornered, misunderstood and get depressed. No one who has learned to be anything in this world is happy for long with their achievements.

What is the world in you?
The world is what you have learned.
To find the truth of life and love is a process of unlearning.
Take for instance love. Everyone on earth today has learned how to love. So when the time comes to really love you have to unlearn what the world has taught you. And that is the pain, the dying to the world, that you feel when your lover fails you or your heart is broken.

I help you to unlearn. I dismantle what the world teaches by exposing what is unnatural and untrue in the world and in your life. That is disturbing and painful as you reach through the pieces towards the truth of yourself. But I am here to help you overcome the world. The pain you can handle; the world you can't.

THE INTELLECTUAL PATH

In truth there are no methods.

ALL METHODS ARE on an outward course, moving away from the simple being of the body now.

Truth is obvious – here and now in my own experience. It is being in my body, not out of it; being in my senses, not in my brain.

I teach a way of being. I do not teach the intellect. Intellectualism is any attempt to leave, ignore or escape my body. It is every need to know something other than the natural simplicity of being.

For instance, intellectual love is avoidance or ignorance of the ground of love between man and woman. It may appear to be an unselfish and unconditional love, but it cannot be made real, or realised, without immersion in the condition of love, in the selfish or personal love that is central to the love of man and woman for each other's bodies. Only by willingly entering and addressing this condition is it possible to enter the sense of love, or pass through into the body of impersonal love. Avoiding this ground of love, it is impossible to fully realise the field of love, which is God-consciousness.

That is why no intellectual method can reach the reality of God. In intellectual reflection God has no place, and disappears.

ART AND THE SPIRIT

The great art is in being.

ART IS NOT exclusive. Like truth, it is all-embracing, all-inclusive. Art is not artiness with all its absurd pretensions and exclusivity. Neither does true art require us all to be doers. We can't all be sculptors, actresses, writers. The appreciation and love of art in any form, including the youthful enthusiasm of being a fan or a follower, is as important as doing or making art, for without one there would not be the other. Who plays to an empty theatre or paints for no one to see?

You must see that the artist's work is purely self-expression. Appreciation, interest, love of art – just as love of anything or anyone – is all self-expression. All men and women, artists and non-artists, are equal at this point of common humanity.

The pleasure and satisfaction of art is not in 'doing' but in the knowledge of the doing; and that can be either in painting the picture or in appreciating it. This knowledge arises from the ground of sensation that is in every body. But once we identify with the knowledge – make it 'mine' – the sensation becomes a personal feeling and acquires individual personal past, with different degrees of emotional intensity. The sensation may be of an energy that is about to take artistic form. Or it may be appreciation, or enthusiasm. But if I invest it with a personal feeling, such as pride or resentment, it becomes a form of selfish expression. Feelings are our self-existence. While we continue to feel something we exist as that feeling.

The distinction between feelings and sensation is like the difference between artfulness and art. The spiritual teacher's job is to help you make the distinction in your own body. Self-knowledge is getting to know your feelings – discovering the harmonics of your personal keyboard. But more important, it is knowing the difference between the changeable personal feelings, which always refer to something in the past or future, and the sensation in the ground of being, which is always present – like now.

From what I've been saying it can be seen that art is at its finest in each of us before it differentiates into artforms, appreciation, personal interests or enthusiasms; in other words, while it remains at the level of sensation. Here is the being that you must eventually discover in all its power and potential.

Is that being – your being – the only being?

Could it possibly be that there is no other? That the sensation you have in your being is the same sensation that everyone has in their being? If so, it must mean that in billions of different bodies all over the earth there is only the one being. Could that then be the divine being?

This is a wonderful mystery that everyone sooner or later has to solve. The point at which this quest becomes the abiding passion and interest is where the spiritual life, or the 'way', begins in real earnest; and all other forms of self-expression, or art, then become subordinate or incidental to the search for this truth.

SELF-GROWTH AND THE SPIRIT

Therapy takes time; and gives you time.

MANY OF THE men and women who come to me have been involved in some aspect of the self-growth movement, through workshops, groups, therapies, counselling and the like. Few are aware of the essential distinction between self-growth and the spirit. Perhaps I can make the distinction clearer and remove some of the mystification from the subject.

You can grow in self – which is the burden of ordinary selfish life. And you can grow in understanding. But you cannot grow in spirit. This is because you are already spirit, now, in the deepest reaches of your being – in the unconscious. To descend consciously into that pristine state of yourself while still alive, to realise it without the possibility of ever being separate from it again, is the unconscious motivation of all human endeavour. If you are attracted towards either self-growth activities or the spiritual life, it means you are consciously aware of this fundamental urge in yourself.

The question is: What makes your descent into the unconscious so hard and so long? What is it that stands in the way? The answer is: your subconscious.

At the deepest level of your being is the unconscious; on top of it is your subconscious; and on top of that is the conscious awareness you are using now. So the subconscious is all that stands between you now and your beautiful being. It consists of everything you think you are, and what you think the world is. It is your living memory.

Behind every single memory is an emotion, the feeling you
had at that time. When you think or are reminded of something, up comes the old emotion. So by thinking (or using your
subconscious) you resurrect the past, live off your old self, and
call it 'you'. This living past, the subconscious, distracts you
from uniting your beautiful being with this moment, now.

There are two means of getting through the subconscious:
the way of the psyche and through the spirit. Let's look at the
psychic way first. But please do not misunderstand the word
'psychic'; it simply describes the action of the human psyche or
mind, which comprises both your conscious and subconscious
awareness. This is your normal, everyday, psychic self – the
'you' who goes to work, plays with the children, perceives the
world and talks and thinks about it. All thought, interpretation
and analysis are activities of the psyche. Self-growth and
self-improvement methods depend on them.

The way of the psyche is as old as the mind itself. It first
surfaced in the awareness of humanity as religious and
philosophic thought. Those ways of thinking have done a job
and remain with us. But they are outdated – because they are
exclusive, and in their exclusivity they have brought dreadful
discord and suffering to the people of the earth. Today the
human psyche resonates to the impersonal and dispersive
dynamic of the Age of Aquarius, which is not exclusive. With
a huge variety of thought and practice, anyone can be an
expert and anyone a student. The fences of religious and
philosophic dogma are down. The search is for self-liberation.
The self-justification and self-forgetfulness of philosophies and
religions have had their day. But still the search takes time. It
can take forever. For the psychic way is the way of time.

While time remains in you – which means, while you are
attached to the past in your subconscious – you have to go the
psychic way. You have to go through the pain and frustration

of time. If you are engaged in self-growth, you want time. You want time to do what you think; to do this workshop, that meditation, this therapy and so on – which all takes time. Because you want time, you get time; and so you are unable to realise the deepest part of your being which is timeless. In spite of wonderful moments of insight and understanding you keep falling back into frustration. You hang on to time while trying to be timeless.

So what are you doing? You are trying to understand yourself. The goal of the psychic way is understanding. Every person alive is engaged in understanding themselves but relatively few have any consciousness of it; and they are the ones whose longing for understanding expresses itself through a religious or philosophic interest, or the pursuit of self-growth. But what is not known on the psychic way is that the spirit, or your beautiful being, cannot be reached by understanding. The need to understand is of the psyche, the human mind, and the spirit is outside the psyche, beyond understanding. The spirit is utterly inaccessible to understanding and thought. You cannot think about the spirit: you only think you can.

The psychic way is like standing with both feet in a bucket and thinking you can lift yourself off the ground by the handle. Yet while you are struggling and sweating, you are slowly realising the truth – that it's impossible. And that is the whole point. Through self-growth you are growing in understanding – understanding the utter limitation of your own mind; that it cannot know the truth. This is the only mystery in the universe to be solved or realised.

What is the limitation of the mind? Time. The mind must always remain in time, always want time, always take time, always have time for one more question – and so it can never be free of time, never be free now.

Once you understand – by seeing now – that the mind is the limitation of time, your awareness passes beyond it, exceeds time and unites with the timeless. Instantly you are one with the spirit, the unconscious, your beautiful being which was never ever limited anyway.

You realise this now and in every succeeding moment, which is the eternal now. That is the way of the spirit, which is really no 'way' at all because it is always now. The spirit is now. Life is now. Now is timeless.

But if you cannot realise this now, what can you do?

As time is the only problem, you must practise giving up time. This doesn't mean giving up what you're doing in the world or doing nothing. Time is created by the mind. So you have to resist the mind's demand to make time. It is done now and every moment. You do it by not thinking about yesterday or the last moment – good or bad; not even about the film you just saw. Every aimless thought about the past makes more time.

And you give up talking about the past. Keep your troublesome, wearying mind here, now. You can see the sky, trees, people, buildings? You do not need to think about them to enjoy them, now. You only think you do.

The truth of the spirit eliminates all time. Surrender all your yesterdays, every attachment to the whole lot, now – not tomorrow, not gradually. You are instantly united with your unconscious, the timeless. You are free. There are no more 'ways' for you. You know the truth, are the truth.

I am not describing some beautiful, impossible dream. It is the living truth, the reality in existence. I am in the timeless. I am the timeless. I am united with my beautiful being. I am always what I am. And I am an ordinary man as you are an ordinary man or woman. It can be done. And I am here to help you do it.

157

THE PATH DISAPPEARS

The way is death.

THERE IS NO spiritual path. The spirit, God, and all that is real cannot be reached by any path. Every path takes time. The spirit is here now – timeless.

There is a physical 'outer path' through life which everybody is familiar with. There is also the psychic and psychological 'inner path', which is misnamed the 'spiritual path'. Each path is a different time. The outer is measured in birthdays and years; and the inner is immeasurable. Both lead to death: the physical path to external death which nobody can avoid, and the psychic path to inner death which everybody avoids for as long as possible.

Inner death is the death of the psychological body; or the gradual disappearance of every attachment to the notion of self. At the point of inner death all traces of the path disappear. The path itself is seen as false.

The path is the self. As the self disappears so does the path. Or it can equally be said: as the path disappears so does the self.

If you were to paint your face and frighten yourself in the mirror, it would take time and pain to rub it off again. But then you would see yourself as you are and were before you were silly enough to paint your face in the first place. And that's what the psychic path is like.

The miracle of truth is that death, in truth, is life. Immediately I have died sufficiently to self, I realise the spirit, the impersonal truth. I realise I am the timeless, here, now; as I always am and have been. I see implicitly that the timeless spirit I am was not at the end of the path but always behind it, or preceding it; that I do not need to die to the path unless I am on it.

Simply by giving up my belief in a spiritual path and being divested every moment of my notions of self, I am instantly there, here, united with the timeless.

ON YOGA

The harmony is me, not my position.

YOGA MEANS 'UNION'. But union with what? In the West everyone is discontented, frustrated, wondering, trying, wanting, competing; so everyone is in union with what makes them unhappy. The yoga practice of the West is to accept unhappiness and cope with it. And the whole western world copes very well. In our genius we have invented many, many ways of getting around unhappiness. One way is to go out and have a good meal. Another is to go and practise some form of yoga as a temporary relief.

The truth of yoga is the union of being and matter (or as the West would have it, 'mind and body'). When you rid yourself of everything that matters – all the frustration and disturbance that makes you want to compete, doubt, perform, or satisfy some expectation – then the matter and the being are in union and there is a different consciousness. That is yoga as the entry of my consciousness into the matter of my self, the entry of my intelligence into my physical body, so that there is no longer any distinction between the two. As that intelligence, I am able to look through my eyes and smile: 'This is good. Life is good.' Essentially, the yoga of the East is to demonstrate that union.

In my teaching this is achieved by going through all the frustration and unhappiness acquired since birth, which lies inside the body (no one is ever unhappy outside the body) and underneath all of that, the sullen intransigence of matter itself and its stubborn hostility to any intelligent manipulation. As you enter the body you encounter this resistance with all its fears and frustrations. You doubt it's going to work. You're frustrated. You're endeavouring to be still but you think you should really be doing the shopping. Your imagination keeps soaring off to some place other than where you are. In my teaching the practice is to contain all that restlessness, to pass through your resistance and give up all that stands in the way of being where I am now.

Hatha yoga or the practice of asanas is presented as a means of reaching God. Every art is presented to us, according to our lights, as a means of reaching God. I do not practise postures or need hatha yoga to reach God because I have reached God in this body. But if it is right for you to practise asanas then it is a way to reach God because as you go into the body you will have to go through your resistances.

The various postures will do wonders for you in the beginning, but after a little while you'll be saying, 'When I started it was great. But I've fallen back. I'm making a mess of it.' That's the intransigence of matter: 'I'm not going to let you in any further. You've suffered enough to get in this far – but now you're really going to have to work!' And it's then that you feel the resistance of your unhappiness, and a dreadful impatience: 'I think I'll skip the class this week.'

Impatience always finds a perfectly justified excuse, but you have to know that your resistance is trying to keep you out of the body. So you have to go to the class. Don't think about it. Do it. There's only one way to do hatha yoga and that's to do the asanas. But note the seething impatience that wants to do something else, wants to make you think about something else.

When hatha yoga is practised rightly it offers a means to come to terms with frustration, wanting and trying – the barrier to entering the body and finding peace within. It's no good going along to the class as a duty or because you've paid for it, because you want friendship, or because you want to get better at it or do more and more of it. All that is competitive and frustrating – wanting and trying. It pushes you out of the body, not into it. If you want to practise hatha yoga, go and do it – as long as you do not try. And only as long as you love it.

Impatience is projection of your self. In my teaching you practise giving it up by pulling back and withdrawing from the projection, for example as the need to pick up the telephone to make a useless call just because you feel lonely. That only feeds your restlessness so that you have to pick up the phone again tomorrow.

Impatience says either 'It's hopeless. I can't do it,' or 'It's got to happen. I've got to do it now.' But if you're not doing it, then it can't be done now. Do it; or if you can't, give up your impatience.

Give up your impatience with your mum and dad. Give up your frustration with your job. If you don't get yourself right when you're frustrated, you'll never be a real yogi.

The body is basically psychic, which means that it is made up of formulations; it takes on forms very quickly. Where intelligence meets resistance there's a psychic field which can quickly start to form structures. A 'psychic egg' forms around us.

Some hatha yoga or breathing practices may be good for breaking up these formulations. We need a few devices to stop the the psychic egg forming, or to break it. But there is the danger of using too much force. To confront the resistance requires what some would call 'concentration', which is really your own presence focused on your body. After a period of concentrated confrontation with matter, you must have a way of breaking off and being easy. The idea is to have harmony in everything.

Harmony is in me, not the asana. A backbend is not done for the backbend. It is for when you break off and find a greater harmony or more beauty. That beauty is immediately available in me as my own harmony, my own dance within. I am that – because I have no unhappiness in me.

Asanas are a means, not an end. I am the end.

As intelligence enters matter, or I enter my body, there has to be a certain equilibrium. Not too much pressure and yet just enough presence. It is this balance which brings union.

If you stay present, where the intelligence is and where the resistance is, then you can give up the restlessness or impatience, which keeps saying: 'Oh come on, give in to the pain. Give up.' You say, 'This discomfort, this pain, represents a position in my self, or a physical place where the matter has not yet been entered. But I am right up against it.' You remain aware that your intelligence is up against the resistance of the matter inside the body; and every moment you know how far to go. There's no 'trying' in you. You say: 'That hurts. But it's right – a right suffering. I'm not pushing too hard. I know what I'm doing. I'm entering my body. And it's good, or the good is here.'

Then you pull back. Break off when the time is right. Move the body. Don't maintain a position beyond the point where you know it's right to break off. Listen to your body. Listen to your intelligence.

Nevertheless there is a time for discipline. You've got to have discipline in any form of practice. But there also comes a time when you have to look and see, 'Is this right for me?' Once it is demonstrated to you that it's not, do not persist. You might try again later, but you must not persist in what is not right. Your body tells you what is right for you. The body is the truth.

The enjoyment of my body indicates what is right for me. The body is my consciousness, and I am in complete union with it. This is the highest truth I can endeavour to communicate to you. And it is not found through pursuing any practice. Truth is found only through negation. In the pursuit of hatha yoga, for instance, you find the truth of it by negating the trying in you. It is the same with every practice. This applies to everyone in every situation.

Whatever your spiritual practice, you have to integrate it into the entire life, because that is harmony. As you get your life right, so harmony begins to seep right through it. Then you will be the yoga – walking down the street or going shopping. Back home you put the shopping down and are moved to do some asana or other; and the dinner still gets cooked. There's no problem, because everything is sweet and easy. This is real yoga.

The virtue in the practice of asanas is to pursue the excellence of it, whatever that might mean. And you can't know what it means because 'excellence' is unknown, abstract. All you know is that you want to do your best. So you pursue it as a practice, enjoy it, love it and perhaps end up teaching it to others. Then, through teaching, you bring greater objectivity and knowledge to your own practice.

The teacher has to be able to observe what's happening in the student's body – to simply see straight and true. As the teacher looks at the body outside, he also looks within at his own body. That is what it means to look 'objectively'. That's what I do when I am the teacher. I actually look very, very deeply inside my own body as I look at the person in front of me. And this provides the necessary reflection. The teacher enters two bodies at once – his own and the student's. Eventually, both end up being me, the observed. Of course if there is emotion or consideration in the space between teacher and student, neither the truth nor the fact can be seen objectively. But when this objectivity is lived in the whole life, in the body, it can be applied to anything in life.

The question arises: 'Yoga teachings are grounded in traditional Indian philosophies. What real value do these teachings have for the West today?'

The answer is: They have an intellectual value and a value as social entertainment. The only thing that has any reality is the pursuit of God, or self-discovery which is towards God. But to try to attain anything, such as trying to reach God – by whatever means – is wilfulness. To be with God is a matter of giving up your wilfulness through surrender to God's will.

Eastern teachings draw people in the West who are attracted by abstractions and think they're going to get it easy. The teachings of the East induce a feeling of euphoria and appear relatively effortless to follow; but what's the good of an abstract heaven? Among western students of eastern teachings you will find there is generally frustration, trying and wanting; and the feeling that they have not achieved as much as they've heard can be achieved.

People say they follow these teachings as a means to enlightenment. If that is so there must be some enlightened people about, but I've travelled quite a bit around the world and I don't see them. The pursuit of enlightenment is not the truth. You have to be enlightened now. And I'll repeat how you get enlightened now: you give up your impatience, your wanting and trying to be enlightened. You give up and enter this body, this being, now; and know that it is good here – no unhappiness, no pain, just beauty and harmony.

You can read about eastern yogis who are able to suck water up through the anus, or pull their bowels out and wash them. That's great stuff to read about, but it's got nothing to do with enlightenment, with finding the ever-present good,

165

the true, the wondrous beauty that is within the body now.

The weakness of eastern teachings is their tradition – because tradition is the past. Tradition is a little duck on a piece of string that we pull along behind us as we repeat what masters of past ages have said. They are not the master of our age. Their words have been repeated by people who were not masters, and so have become degraded. Even when a living master repeats a tradition, though it is done with a sense of rightness, it's still corrupted by repetition. All tradition is corrupt.

The error of these teachings is to have made truth fit tradition. Eastern teachings look back to an earlier, more harmonic age that cannot be made to fit our times. If you are being taught within a tradition, give up trying to make your own experience fit in with it. Throw out the tradition and keep your own self-experience so that reality can come through to you. If you are practising hatha yoga, use the system you've been taught and do your best; but don't worry about what any of it means. Then what you need to do will be revealed to you.

No tradition: that is my teaching.

Whenever an eastern master talks of tradition he confuses the western mind. Yet it is good to be with the master. It always pays to be with the master of anything you are practising. So if you're doing hatha yoga, it is good to be with the master of yoga; not because someone says he is a master but because it is demonstrated in your own experience that he is the master – he knows what he's doing and what he's talking about.

In the practice of any yoga teaching remember that 'yoga' means union with the good. The master says: 'I am united with the good, the beauty of life inside me now and every moment without cessation. But I am not special. I am an ordinary human being. And it is the right of every human being to unite with the same beauty, wonder and goodness now.'

This is not the goodness that gives gifts to people or writes thankyou letters. It is the goodness that I can be in my body, and which is my own self-knowledge. Yoga is union with that. If you just want to read about it, as beautiful as it sounds, you're never going to reach it. If you just want to talk about it, you're not going to be it. To be it, you have to do it; stop talking about it and do it. Use whatever means, but discover the good inside you. For the good is the beginning of God; only the beginning, for then it becomes love, and then delight, joy, wonder, glory and knowledge of the truth, for the good is always accompanied by truth. And in the great light of that goodness is the enlightened state of pure being.

SANNYAS AND THE DIVINE LIFE

It is not love of the master to call him mine.

'SANNYASIN' IS A Hindi word for someone so devoted to the divine life that he or she has given up all attachments. Recently the term has been popularised in the West to describe followers of the eastern master Bhagwan Rajneesh [later called Osho]. Many of these people also come to my meetings, bringing their attachments with them.

I am here to break all attachments; to break the heart of any sannyasin worthy of having his or her heart broken.

What I say is the truth. I do not go round the world talking to the people for them to believe in me or worship me. I speak as I do to have my truth destroyed; and if you can't destroy my truth, then hear it and learn from it, for until my truth is destroyed I am the living truth.

The master of the sannyasins is the truth. There is no doubt about the master. When they are in his presence they are in the best of company. But that's not enough. As soon as sannyasins leave the master, they start looking for instruction in their own heads. If they could hear the truth of the master they would do what the master says. The sannyasins who come before me do not do as the master says. And that's cheating.

Anyone who is in the company of the master and is receptive to the truth will register the tremendous truth in themselves and the partial dropping of their burden. That is purifying. But the way Rajneesh teaches is no good to me. I can say this because I am teacher of the West. The teacher of the East cannot teach the West. He can inform you and his presence can illumine the truth in you beautifully. But what's the good of that? I am already illumined – in every body. The illumined one is not the problem in your body. It's your self that's the matter. And that self is cultured in the West, meaning it's cunning, devious, easily seduced and not willingly mastered. People in the West require instruction. They must be told how to get their life right, especially their love-life.

Someone encased in the western mind is incapable of receiving the stillness of the East, represented in the serene face of the eastern master. The eastern way of coping with the world is complete detachment. The East is serenity, passivity, stillness. The West is attachment, sex and insanity. The stillness of the East can't handle it. To live the truth in the western world requires tremendous presence.

It is of the East to prostrate oneself on the ground before the master and give him glorious titles and to worship him as God. But you of the West cannot live such devotion. You are easily deluded by the glamour of the God-man. Any man who tells you he is God is a bullshitter. The master is not God. Never let that be said. For either all men are God or none is. Some men have been reduced to nothing and have realised such purity that they reflect the immediate presence or beauty and wonder of God to themselves and to others. But no man is God.

The master is the living truth and you have to hear his truth. If it is the truth for you, that is what stirs the living truth in your body. And that is what decides your direction. It is no good listening to priests. Beware of a master or a teaching that is surrounded by priests – or therapists, or any intermediaries. There is only one master where I am, only one teacher in this truth and one expression of it. Barry Long speaks for Barry Long. When I am gone, I am gone forever – never to be seen again. But when the master is gone, the

169

priests crawl like maggots out of his body and try to speak the truth that only he can speak.

Sannyasins tend to live in 'spiritual communities' which is an idea the East has injected into the West. It can't work. It's not a practical way of living the divine life. It is the resort of desperation with the western world. When the master is not there the people go to sleep. They become friends and have nice discussions about the truth – instead of being it. I ask you, how can anyone ever discuss the truth?

Be very careful of having friends in the spiritual life. They are likely to listen without complaint to your sad, sad story; and then instead of serving you they will indulge your own indulgence in emotion. A true friend does not just soak it up for you. A true friend is there to serve you in truth, which means he or she will do something for you that works.

Whatever works, the practical, is what we need in the West. The western mind is practical. The East did not make the motor car or the microphone. The westernised mind made the world through analysing, categorising and the invention of practical science. There's no love in science; because love is of the East. What happens when man and woman in the West look East is that the practicality and the love get mixed up. To keep things straight the teaching of truth in the West must be practical. Start with the practical first; that leads back to love.

So what is the practical truth of friendship? If you start with love – in the form of being nice, kind, polite, trying to love – you will get confused; because friendly love doesn't get results. The practical basis of friendship is loyalty. I am loyal to those who have served me, as I am loyal to my mother who sacrificed herself for me. I am loyal to my father who went to work to put the butter on my bread. I am willing to serve that which serves me. To know this removes all confusion over friendship; and in relation to mother and father or anyone who confuses your love by making demands on it – 'You owe me . . . I'm your mother.' No. I owe you nothing. But inasmuch as you have served me, I am loyal to that; and in my loyalty I will take what practical action I can to serve you. Then I may know my love of you.

Sannyasins usually take on new names, given by their master, and wear special clothes to mark them out. This is supposed to shake the mad western world out of them. Rajneesh turned everything upside down for his followers; and in the 1970s he really terrified their parents, or that generation in the West that was shocked to see young people wearing orange robes in the streets of western cities, who wanted to laugh at what was happening to their children but couldn't because they were so terrified. Rajneesh gave those people in the West a real shaking. It had to be done. But everything that was new yesterday is old hat today. Sannyasins became like the flower people of the 1960s, getting older and older but not getting anywhere; their style of life as ridiculous as that of any other cult.

Everything that is new today becomes dead tomorrow, and joins the vicious circle in which humanity runs round and round, never getting anywhere. Since you take the treasure of yesterday as if it were the treasure of today, which it is not, eventually the living truth must take everything you have treasured; and in return give you nothing.

What do you look for in a master? Do you look for anything more than the truth? Do you want someone to worship? Some ceremony? A crucifix glowing on the wall? A pretty dress? What do you want?

How man and woman love the ceremony, the carnival! But there's no carnival now – unless in the midst of the carnival you can glory in the beauty of all that is now, the wonder of God, without any attachment to the last moment. Can you just love life and say 'I am not attached?' For love has no attachments.

What is your attachment? Is there a feeling in you at this very moment? A feeling of resentment, doubt, anger? Anything that drums away inside or needles you or makes you restless is your attachment.

Can you feel an attachment in you? Then be it – without letting your mind have a dialogue with it. For that is the truth working.

I ask western sannyasins with oriental names: Can you change your name back again and live as an ordinary man or woman in the West? Or are you going to remain special? Are you a man who wears his collar back to front to mark him out as godly? Are you going to remain a member of some cult? Or are you an ordinary being, able to be with the people and walk through the ignorance of the world without it touching you?

How long are you going to need a pack of cards to entertain yourself with?

The robes and beads have to go. If the master gave you an ornament or image of him to wear, it is a pale reflection of the bead of reverence you have inside you: 'I know what I have received from you, master, and I am grateful for it.' That is enough. Your gratitude to the master is the most beautiful thing, the repayment in love and presence of his service to you.

There are very few masters in the body on this earth and they all know what they're doing. That's their extraordinary quality: you can tell where the master is, because the man knows what he's doing. But no master has any existence whatsoever in his own right, for he is only the reflection of the one master which is God. And so it is that God leads man from one place of reflection to another. In the presence of the living master you always receive the extraordinary energy of that presence, by which you know him. But always look to see what it is to be a master, so that in time or the next moment you can be the master.

ASCENDED MASTERS

A revelation of ignorance.

YOU WILL PROBABLY have heard of Ascended Masters and long-dead entities that use living people to channel their teachings. These 'psychic masters' and spirit-teachers are half-masters. A half-master is not the master, just as a half-truth is not the truth. A psychic half-master is neither master enough nor truth enough to be responsible for his own body here and now. He takes over some other body by psychic possession, maintaining that he is free of the body, which is true, but which is also a lie since he finds it necessary to possess one.

No one is as misguided, misleading or cunningly adept as the disembodied psychic half-master – the 'Ascended One', he of the 'White Brotherhood' and the like – no one, that is, except for the disembodied half-master of the Black Brotherhood, which the Ascended White Brother in his ignorance and half-truths (or half-lies) necessarily creates.

Psychic half-masters are invariably priest-like presences. Each in his own time or body did in fact live with and was directly instructed by a living spiritual master of his tribe or people.

A priest is a self-perpetuating, self-appointed quasi-spiritual lieutenant. He is not the master because he has not realised the truth of the master by living it. And the truth of the master is this: The master does not return. Only the priest posing as a spiritual master or spirit-teacher comes back. He has to come back – to reveal his ignorance. That is the divine justice or joke of it. His presence is his own rebuttal.

When you realise, by dying, that there is no death, you will know as much in your own way as these psychic priests. Since you will be in the psyche freed of the impediment of physical consciousness, you too will be able to look forward and back in time into the future and past. You will have an inconceivable advantage over the living. But perhaps, after reading this, you will be more real than those ancient priests; and you will not return to add your burden to human confusion.

The tragedy of the psychic priest, for himself and everyone, is that he doesn't know that he doesn't know. He firmly believes in himself and in what he's doing. Indeed, he does have a power of presence. This comes from having been next to the living master in his time or body, and not just a blind follower. This implies true worthiness that is earned, not given. Over and over he heard the truth from the master's lips. But instead of living it he busied himself converting it into memorable knowledge, into intriguing priestly forms, systems of mystification and marvellous esoteric revelations – which he continues, even centuries later, to espouse as truth.

Today, the psychic priest's knowledge from another time is enormously impressive, and supernaturally convincing due to his magical ability to communicate to the living as a psychic presence through another's body. But none of what he teaches or says is the truth. Nor does it lead anyone to the truth.

The living master never returns. He teaches the truth he is in his own body, his own time. When that is finished, all that he had to say and do is said and done. If it weren't, he would not die.

The body is the precise time allotted. There can be no return of J Krishnamurti, Meher Baba, Ramana Maharshi or any living master of his time. The master never needs more time.

After death the master goes on where none but the master can follow. Everyone goes on who is not held back by the priests, for there is a place for everyone who goes on. What this place is can only be known in the stillness and silence of death. But ignorance cannot go on. So it stays or returns to reveal its folly.

For a time after the death of the living master's body (or anyone you love) his presence may vibrate in those who have loved him for the truth he taught and is. During that period he may be perceived psychically within or without. But the communication will be very simple and to this effect: 'I am here now and forever. Always I am with you. Do not fear, all is well. Be still.' Nothing more complicated or erudite. And not long after, all communication as that presence will cease, except for love.

The descending Ascended Ones obtain possession of bodies by lying in wait for someone who is willing to accept a seductively proffered invitation to let them in and play the psychic game; someone whose consciousness is actually nearing the potential of attracting a living master. At this time the person concerned is acutely receptive; but also highly vulnerable to mistaking inner psychic displays of magic or knowledge for spiritual truth, and mistaking the accompanying psychic presence for that of the master.

Possession invariably begins with an impressive psychic demonstration through the person. The astonished subject realises this could not be of their own doing or consciousness. They write, draw, act or speak in a way that amazes them; and then amazes others.

One of these priest-identities, calling himself Djwhal Khul, or The Tibetan, used the body of Alice Bailey through automatic writing and many books of lofty teaching were produced. A central theme was the denunciation of glamour. But this limited priestly perception failed to see that the ultimate glamour is psychic magic – the trick of securing entry into a body or consciousness that is not one's own and then controlling it in the name of the good.

Unlike the living master, the possessing identity will not allow the person to realise the truth of themselves – the unity I am in every body. The two of them will be coming and going in the one body until it dies, or until it loses its usefulness as a mouthpiece or channel.

Dispossessing a living person (a channeler) of a genuinely powerful psychic priest can only be done through the intelligence of the entity, not the person. The entity must hear the truth of the master and face it honestly. He must voluntarily withdraw from the person's consciousness by going on, as he should have done long ago. Then the master can come.

Until now the Ascended Masters have not had this reflection from a living master. Living masters have either denied their existence or ignored them; or disowned them as J Krishnamurti did. After realising the truth he dumped the whole ascended crew on the Theosophical Society like a ton of hot bricks.

Here is my message to the Ascended Masters:

'Are you listening, Kuthumi, Djwhal Khul, Morya, Maitreya, Archangel Michael, Serapis, Hilarion, Ramtha and the rest of your kind? I'm speaking to you – you who occupy a place in the human psyche called limbo, but do not know it. You, who are intelligent enough to hear, have drawn the master to you again – he whom you know knows where you are, what you are and what you are doing, as always.

'You must go on. You must go on because you have heard the truth. You must withdraw, even though it is the death of you. You must die for the truth, which you did not do in your own body, in your own time. That's why you are not the master and did not know the truth of the master. A master is he who has died for the truth in his own body, his own time. 'Until now you could not die. Centuries and ages are irrelevant in limbo. To be meaningful, death has to occur or be realised in a physical body. But you have had no body of your own; you've been stealing them. You can only die by facing the truth of the living master, the truth you did not face in your own time. Only the living master can reach you; for only he is above you.

'Now, through possessing a living body you have the chance to die for the truth in it; another chance to go on. If you accept the opportunity, the body will have been given to you for this purpose and no karma will be attached to it – no price to pay. If you do not, the body you're using will not have been given; it will have been taken by you for your own selfish and ignorant ends, and by the law of life, karma or justice you must pay for it. What that means you will either already know or must learn.

'You must announce in the body you are using that you have heard the truth of the living master and you are going on. You must tell the people only this, and be gone.'

THE INNER VOICE

Some speak of an inner voice that guides them.

INNER VOICES OCCUR on the psychic path. They range from utterances of sheer nonsense and dangerously misleading advice to amazingly accurate prophecy and statements of sublime wisdom.

As the man or woman willingly and valiantly dies psychologically, facing the circumstance of life, so the voices reduce in number and sound.

As the stillness deepens from the dying of self, the voice of truth may speak, but not necessarily.

Do not look for a voice. Looking can attract the lower psychic and misleading voices. What is true will always come of itself when you are ready, when you have created enough space and silence for it by dying to your attachment to your self – as best you can, without frustration or trying.

All voices cease when the timeless is the state of consciousness. The reason is that in the timeless divine mind there is no separation, no distance, no question. There is no delusion that there is anything to know but the reality of life – here, now. In that all knowledge is implicit and the divine gnosis is once more heard in the world.

EXTRA-SENSORY PERCEPTIONS

Only being in the senses makes sense.

IF YOU COULD learn to speak to dolphins, what could you tell them of value that they don't already live and know? Do they need to know Einstein's theories or how to carry a torpedo? How would you excuse your boredom to these intelligent, liberated creatures?

When you're down, would you tell them your sad story and make them unhappy too?

If you eventually manage to converse with extra-terrestrial intelligences, how will you account for your recurring moods, worries and problems? How will you explain that these negative reactions are not actually the way that people on earth have of enjoying themselves?

Would you tell the space-beings that although you are responsible men and women, you are not responsible for your unhappiness – it's foisted upon you? Could you persuade another intelligence that it's intelligent to blame someone or something else for the circumstances of your life?

Would you argue that unhappiness is natural on this planet? Is it not self-evident that nothing natural is unhappy except at the hands of unhappy man and woman?

When you leave off communicating with animals and spirit-beings and go home, how well do you communicate with your partner or children?

THE TRUTH OF CRYSTAL

Are you rock or crystal?

ONE OF THE popular interests today seems to be in crystals. People are hanging them round their necks, looking into them, praying over them, putting them on show. So I'll tell you the truth of crystals.

A crystal was once a rock. Rock is solid, heavy, stuck, dark, immovable. Crystal is a refinement of rock. Crystal reflects the light. A crystal vibrates. Crystals are used to make sound: in the latest science of sound the finest sounds are created through crystals. The crystal resonates: it can be used for telling the time. If you want to, you can handle the crystal to bring about some apparently magical effect. Sometimes it will work; sometimes it won't – so that can't be the truth of crystal.

The point of crystals is for you, man or woman, to crystallise yourself – to make yourself as pure, as clear as crystal. You can be rock-hard, dull and immovable. Or you can be crystalline, scintillating, resonating to the beauty of life. What is your resonance now? Are you turgid, depressed and burdened like a rock? Or are you sweet and crystal clear? Look inside yourself. Do you have the rock, the burden in you? Or the sweetness of crystal? Can you sense the life inside yourself, the wonder and beauty of it? That's all you need to start to make yourself crystal clear.

There is a place for rock on this earth, and it is good. Everything is good on this earth – rock and crystal – but you must put the rock in its place. The place for rock in your body is down in your stomach, down around your pelvic bones, down there where you sit inside your body – that is the rock, the earthy part of you. So let the rock be heavy, solid. Let the rock be itself there, for that is its place in the earth which your body represents. If you let the rock get into your head – if you let the heaviness creep up there in the form of thinking – you get rock-hard in the brain. And you vibrate to the heavy dirge of thought instead of resonating beautifully with crystal clarity.

The whole of you is crystalline. You are vibrating with life. You are life on earth and the life you hear in the breeze, the birds, the insects, you hear with your crystal consciousness, your crystal-clear being in the body. If you've got rocks in your head, how will you hear anything but the burden of living?

To be real man, real woman, you've got to crystallise yourself. You've got to do it now, by being now. You've got to give up the thought-made burden.

Now, which are you – rock or crystal?

THE ROMANCE OF THE SPIRIT

Do you dare to put the truth in the past?

'Is ANYONE THERE please? Can you hear me? It is I, the spirit of Avalon, speaking. I'm sorry if my voice seems faint and far away. But I'm buried . . .

'You've heard of me, I'm sure. I'm the living spirit of Christianity in Britain. I am the living truth, which they buried in the stories and religion. I am the truth behind the legendary visit of Jesus to Britain, the truth of the location of the Holy Grail and the Arthurian quest. I stand for all that is good and true in the name of Avalon. Indeed I am the spirit behind the name of anything that man and woman love.

'Every day I call out like this. No one seems to hear. Perhaps today someone will.

'The spirit of a thing is your love of it now; and the strength of your love is the strength of your longing.

'I sit at the great round table of the earth and through each seat of longing I am reached. But I am reached only now, as I am heard only now. I am not memorable, not historical. Any connection made to me by your mind is past, dead.

'Why do you look for me in history, but not now? Why do you keep burrowing into the past, and piling the stifling stuff of legend on top of me, when here I am now? Not that I am in any danger. What you do affects you, not me. I am not dead or dying under this muck. Death is just another of your inventions, another silly speculation you've put between us. You believe in death, so you separate yourself from life now.

It is you who are dead. You're living in your own grave, dug out of the past. You are the living dead.

'Where am I buried? Here, where life and truth are buried – in you.'

Avalon, Camelot, Glastonbury, Paradise . . . Just some of the place-names in the human longing for what is good and true. May I tell you the secret of sacred places? May I tell you the secret of Glastonbury, and put you on the way to Paradise?

Glastonbury, as everyone with a sense of presence knows, is not a place, certainly not a town or a hill. Somehow, if you feel the mystery of it, it is living . . . now.

Nor is Glastonbury a legend. A legend can never be true. A legend is a dream, an impossible dream, kept active in the minds of sleeping men and women by their longing. The impossible legend of Glastonbury is the wandering of that longing through the illusions of the past, stepping like a knight of old in the footprints of Jesus, in search of a magical kingdom of justice, purity, valour, love and truth on earth – which can never be.

Such endless longing and dreaming is perpetuated in the sleepers' imagination by poetry, prose, plays and the merry pretence of pageant; in people happy to be sad, like the clown who, as everyone with a sense of presence knows, is the image of a man longing for himself.

Happily or sadly, there is no truth or reality in legend. Like salt water, it just feeds an unquenchable thirst. Legends are dreams. But myth is reality. Glastonbury is myth. Everything it stands for is absolutely real. But Glastonbury never happened, was never real in the past. It is real now.

Legends are the dreams of men. Myth is the stark reality of gods. Would you make a legend, a dream, of the gods too?

Before you do, know this. The gods of all time are none

other than man or woman who has awakened from the dream. That awakening is the continuous shattering of the legend or dream of the past in themselves. In that, they perceive or realise the mystery, the living myth of their longing, re-enacting itself each moment within. There, here, they are freed of the illusions of history, of beginning and end, of comforting presence, doubt, longing and searching; because the mystery that is no mystery but the living truth is before them now in the reality of themselves.

The truth behind all longing awakes when you do; in the shattering of all your dreams. When you are real enough to stand dreamless and alone in Glastonbury, then you are in Paradise.

What New Age Was That?

I'm not coming. I never went.

TALK OF A New Age, of spiritual transformation and higher consciousness on earth, is exciting, absorbing, entertaining; but it is not the truth. As the teacher of truth, I must tell you the truth. There never was and cannot be a New Age of spiritual transformation. Nor is there a New Age for you, the man or woman reading this. The New Age movement is a delusion and any involvement in it or belief that it will assist you in your spiritual development will actually keep you from the truth. You may have a good time, meet knowledgeable and nice people, learn new things and even witness magical effects. You may feel you are making progress. But you will still remain as you are – discussing the truth, believing in it, but not realising it.

New ages are simply successive civilisations, different ways and means of living; making life easier, more interesting and entertaining. New ages come and go, as the men and women who inhabit them come and go.

What comes and goes is not the truth. The truth is now. Now and always.

If there ever was an Atlantis, in which everyone communicated intuitively and travelled by instantaneous solar transport, it passed away into legend. If the New Age dream is ever realised and the people of the earth are united into one consciousness, that new civilisation will again produce just another way of living that will also pass away.

185

What has any Age, past or future, got to do with the good of you, the truth of you, this moment, now?

If there ever is a New Age, or ever was a Golden Age and if there is any truth in the New-ager or Atlantean, that truth is in man and woman now. The truth is that I who am reading this, here and now, am always what I am, irrespective of the time and the place. I go to sleep and I wake in the morning – the same 'I' . . . I am here. I am staying. I am going. I am always something or other. I am always confirming what I am. The circumstances I live in come and go, but I am always present. The comfort and convenience of living changes, but I who long for truth and love am always here, just the same.

If I do not know this, here and now, something is amiss. What is it? How could the truth, the reality of myself, be forgotten?

'I forget it because I am always remembering. I am always looking back, or looking forward. I am always dreaming, imagining, speculating, wishing . . . I have forgotten how to be what and where I am now.'

'I cannot just be here, now. It's boring. I'm restless. I get too unhappy without something to do. Please let me be distracted from my unhappiness. There must be something better, a better tomorrow. I will work towards it. I'll look forward to it.'

And that is the grand delusion of all times.

TEACHINGS ARE RAFTS

Now walk on the water.

EACH TEACHER OR teaching in one's spiritual journey is a raft. You step off one raft in the spiritual stream onto the next. And each time it is a process of profound spiritual change; for each raft has less substance to hold on to than the one before, less to satisfy the mind and emotions, less of what is comfortable, less that can be shared and discussed.

My teaching, when you are ready for it, is sufficient to take you to the great sea, to the vast energetic nothing within, which is everything and into which all disappears – what is.

For those who are not ready, this teaching will have insufficient substance; and they will quickly fall through it to something more substantial – a more popular and under-standable teaching that is more outside themselves; which means it will be more in their heads or in ceremony, more emotionally and mentally memorable.

Know that what is emotional, mental or memorable is not the spirit, not the truth.

To stay in the midstream of truth, and not get distracted or caught up in backwaters, you must always be true to yourself. This means you must listen to all the teachers presented to you by life, rejecting none, and go with the teaching that enables you to be true to yourself now. It must allow you to be true to yourself without any trying, pretending or imagining. This is not likely to be a comfortable option, as I am not talking about selecting or choosing a teacher.

A particular teaching may have helped you very much in past years, and to acknowledge that help is a measure of the love in you. You were led to that teaching. Now you may find yourself withdrawing from it because you cannot make all of that teaching real for yourself now; which means you cannot be true to yourself. So that teaching has done its job. It's no longer for you. No choice is involved. You just can't go on with it. It's as simple as that. That is honesty. That is self-knowledge working without the involvement of the person, the chooser of ignorance.

You cannot love a teaching, or a 'spiritual path', although you may think you do. Your love is God, the eternal. If you perceive or register your love as something or someone that draws you towards that unnameable source, then that is the path to your love for now. But know that your fulfilment is not in the path; it is purely in union with your love.

No 'spiritual path' is easy; or, if it is, you're in a backwater – enjoying yourself and forgetting your love.

In truth, everything is the reverse of how the human mind sees it. The mind perceives through the distorting mirror of emotions stored in the psyche. For example, the stream of truth leading to the great sea of God or nothing is not as your mind would imagine it. It does not flow down towards something else or something that is 'more'. Nor is the stream moving; for it is the person that moves. The seeming movement or progress is the dissolving, or dropping away, of the ignorance that is the person. The stream is not different from the sea, the means not different from the end. When there is no person left, there is neither stream nor sea. Only nothing; or everything.

Your life to this point, and all your previous teachings, have been your preparation for what comes next. You have gone beyond what went before, absorbed all it had to give you. The good it gave you is in you forever, has become you. The awareness it gave you is now what you are. And you will always be grateful for that.

Now here you are, on the next part of the path to God, your love, your true being that shines beneath the falsehood of your emotions and your thinking, imagining mind. Understandably, you may still be holding on to something of the old and questioning the new. And your questioning is right. That is why I endeavour to help you distinguish between the old and the new.

For a long time the spiritual life seems to be a matter of expanding personal consciousness. But really the whole process is being able to dip into or enter the consciousness that is already there – in the first instance the consciousness of the teaching provided and sustained by the living master.

My teaching is a flow of consciousness on earth, an energetic stream of original teaching. My responsibility is to keep the stream pure. Those who are with me at any time can dip into it, or dive into it. It is there to be used, as all who use it contribute to it.

A spiritual teaching is simply that: a stream of consciousness evolving in power and purity through the struggles, sacrifices and devotion to the truth of those moved by it, and preserved by the clarity and simplicity of the presence or teaching of the master. All serve the stream, as all are served by it. And all this by the grace of God.

THE WAY NOW

*The way of the spirit
is really no 'way' at all
because it is always now.
It goes nowhere.
It is always here
now.*

THE MIRROR OF TRUTH

What does not change? See that and see the truth.

THE TRUTH IS now. It does not change.

The world is a place of apparently ceaseless change.

To see the truth that does not change I must first look for it in the world of change. This requires the steadiness that comes from having lived enough in the world, from having loved and suffered enough, succeeded and failed enough; so that I am not carried away by the world's passing attractions.

As the truth does not change, the truth of the world is what never changes in the world. And what is that? What in the world is the same today as always? That is the question for you to answer.

But first, take a look into the mirror of truth. For although a mirror is not the truth, it reveals the truth.

The mirror of truth is the world of ceaseless change. As you look into it you see the things that come and go; but you overlook the bigger picture, or what does not change. It is the same with a bathroom mirror. If I see only particular reflections, such as my image, or a pimple, obviously I am not looking at the whole picture, the truth of it all.

So what is the truth of a mirror? I will tell you in a moment, and you will recognise it as soon as I say it, but for now the point is that you are distracted by the particulars; the image of yourself in the mirror, the pimples, the thoughts.

The truth of a mirror is that everything in it is reversed. Left is right; writing is back to front. This never changes. Nothing in the mirror is as it is in reality. That's the truth of mirrors.

So, what is the same in the world today as it always was? Everything in the world comes and goes, and has been coming and going since the mythic Eden – except for one thing that has not changed. It is that I continue to be unhappy. This is the truth of the world. Whenever it suits me, I continue to assail the earth and everyone around me with my moods, doubts, resentments, disappointments, impatience, bitterness, frustration, guilt, anger, grief, fear and sorrow. As I look into the mirror of the world, so happy am I to be unhappy that I refuse to put an end to my selfish self-expression; and so I continue refusing to take responsibility for my self.

I want to be saved from my unhappiness and irresponsibility, but all the searching for higher consciousness, all the teachings, the presence of countless masters, sages, saints, philosophers, adepts and initiates has made not the slightest difference. I still long to be fulfilled. I am still searching for the truth, waiting for a new age to dawn, for a saviour, for a fundamental change that never comes.

Whatever will do the trick? Perhaps I could learn to dematerialise and psychically transport myself elsewhere in the universe. But what would I do when I arrived to find that my unhappiness had re-materialised with me? —just as it does in this world and this body. Perhaps I could learn to work magic, or walk across burning coals. But would that change anything? No, a nameless fear would still arise in me at night.

So what's gone wrong in existence? What on earth has happened? You have climbed into the mirror. And in the mirror you are unable to see the truth of it, or why the world appears to be a crazy, mixed-up, unhappy place.

The error is that you should not be there at all. You are the flaw in the glass. Your presence there is distorting the reflection. When you remove yourself from the mirror the whole reflection of the world is immediately different. Consciousness is transformed.

You have to climb out of the mirror. But how?

First, you have to know what you are doing. All I can do is tell you what it's like to be stuck in the mirror. You have to see if it's the truth.

As you look about you in the mirror, everything is either coming or going. You are the only permanent feature. So nothing around you is dependable. This makes you insecure, uncertain and often confused. The more insecure and confused you are the deeper into the mirror you go, looking for something that will endure; but everything comes and goes, even fame, failure and success. You try to hold on to things, but the harder you try the more you are hurt when they slip away. The hurt makes you feel vulnerable so you put on a veneer of hardness or weakness. The stress gets worse. You know you are somehow out of place and sometimes you see with great clarity that you are only a shallow image of yourself. You go on trying to hold your mirror-world together and shove your hurts and disappointments away from view, out of conscious awareness. But subconsciously the ferment of tension coils like a spring inside you. This drives you ambitiously, competitively, blindly round and round the vicious circles of the mirror-world. Coping in this madhouse you forget how unhappy you are; but you never quite forgive yourself.

I am the truth outside the mirror. You like to call the truth I am 'your higher self'. This is an excuse for not being what you are, where you are. There is no higher self, no lower self.

There is only the self in the mirror and I who am looking at it. I am intelligence. My intelligent reflection – my body – is in the mirror, in the world, but I remain timelessly out of it, because I am not attached to the comings and goings of my reflection.

You must detach from your self and join me, where I am. I cannot step out of the mirror for you, because you are the one inside it. As the teacher of truth I can only confirm for you the truth you have always known: nothing in the world that you can think of or look to is the truth.

I also have to warn you that the mirror's power of illusion is great. As you endeavour to clamber out of it you will look for support. The nearest things available will be your thoughts, doubts and fears. If you hold on to them you will become as unsteady and wavering as they are. Then you may look for stronger support elsewhere, in other teachings perhaps, that will allow you more time, more reflections, more dreams. In your uncertainty you may try to block the way out for yourself and endeavour to destroy the truth I am. You may seek to protect your position, your unhappiness, by thinking that I am in the mirror too. In your doubt and fear you will do your utmost to drag the truth, your salvation, down into the mirror, your delusion.

THE LIVING TRUTH

You come to me to enlighten the brain.

THERE IS ONLY one truth. It is being where you are; and where you are, is where your body is.

This is too simple for the brain to comprehend in its now chronically complicated condition. The brain has become so divided in itself and burdened with problems that the truth – the living truth, or living the truth – no longer has any real meaning for it. When the brain does attempt to find the truth it gets stuck in its own contrived religious or scientific dogmas and becomes even more divided, confused and confusing.

No matter how preoccupied you are at any time with thinking, wishing, dreaming or worrying, you will always wake up or return to consciousness in the living reality of your body. In fact, it can be said that in all the psychological activity you've ever engaged in, you didn't go anywhere or do anything. You only thought you did. It all happens in the brain, not in reality.

(Again you'll notice the brain's inability to grasp what I've just said; and its urge to argue or dismiss the statement.)

The only way to get around the ignorance of the brain is for you to live the truth. Living it means doing it, not thinking about it.

You have to make the brain simple again, return it to its natural simplicity. You have to strip it of its acquired and treasured ignorance. You have to restore it to the innocence of being one with your body here and now. In this state of innocence, of rediscovered union, all is made wondrously simple, like yourself, your life and the whole apparent, complicated world of problems around you.

You come to me, the living master, to learn how to do this, to learn how to 'be' again. You come to me to practise being – being simple, being simply where you are, where your body is. I cannot do it for you. I simply show you how.

You come to discover that there is only one 'me'. And it is the same intimate presence of being that each one refers to as 'me' – not my self, not my unhappiness, not the world in me, but the living reality of every body.

Your body is the physical cross you've drawn for yourself in the square of space and time.

The body marks your unique and unalterable place in existence. This is the unarguable reality which the brain can't realise, can't make real. But the consciousness behind the brain can.

The brain is always striving to be somewhere or somebody else – wanting to change, wanting to improve, wanting to want. It gets bored and restless very quickly with being where the body is. But the consciousness behind the brain – its intelligence – is steady, unwavering and in constant delightful union with the body.

In fact it is the consciousness behind the brain now that is illuminating your physical body with the sense of well-being. This illumination is common to all the earth's creatures. But only man and woman choose to lose touch with it. Of all the species they alone forget and leave this glowing, ever-present intelligence.

It is consciousness that knows, loves and enjoys life in the physical body, even while the brain agonises in thought-full depressions or considers suicide.

You come to be with me to enter your body, to bring the steady state of consciousness forward. In other words, you come to enlighten your brain. Uninterrupted enlightenment of the brain was once the natural state of man and woman. The brain was a perfect physical instrument. It served the consciousness of man and woman and the will of the earth. Nothing suffered from its activities. Today the instrument has taken over. The servant has usurped the master's role. And the earth and every creature on it are victims of the brain's mad and irresponsible wilfulness.

Due to the ignorance of our times, or the sophisticated brain, uninterrupted enlightenment is now one of the earth's great rarities. It is almost an extinct phenomenon, comparable physically to the planet's most endangered (by the brain) species.

And so it is said, the earth has few living masters.

BEING HUMAN BEINGS

The master is not human.

WHAT IS A human being? How do we recognise one?

A human being, or being human, is the unquestionable right (which is therefore the unquestioned right) to sacrifice life daily to the love of being worried, depressed, confused, sad, frustrated, ambitious, guilty, angry, moody, resentful, impatient and thoughtful, and to believing and not believing. In other words, it is the right to be happy one moment and unhappy the next.

Being human, a human being is unreliable; like a rotting bridge that may or may not collapse under you at any second.

Do you recognise the human who's spoiling it all, spoiling it for you? Do you recognise the spoiler – not in someone else, but in you?

Human beings are wilful beings. To be wilful is to persist in choosing to follow one's own painful, unhappy path. To be willing is to receive the truth now; receive it simply by doing and being.

The living master is provided to help you remove the human from the being; to show you how to do it; how to be, by being now. For it is God's pleasure that you enjoy your life, your being – when you've had enough of the wilful human spoiler you love and sacrifice your life to.

The human brain is a terrible master, and everyone has one. The brain must be reduced to having one impulse. While it has two it plays between them, and plays up. When it has several impulses, or preoccupations, it makes a game of the individual's life. Those who are devoted to the truth (as the master) can be saved from the human brain; meaning that I, as the master, can keep the human brain at bay, even at a distance, through the individual's one-pointed impulse towards me. This impulse is an in-pulse, incessantly pulsing in the sensation of being. It is the one-pointedness of devotion to truth, life, God.

This one and only impulse, this profound inner pulse, is what I know I love. What I know I love (if I have been fortunate enough for it to have been revealed to me) is what I know I want forever and ever without cessation. I know it because it is in my living sensating experience.

We can only want one-pointedly what we already know. And it must be known substantively or it will escape us – escape from our purity – escape with us into the imagination of the brain. Then the brain lives on as the terrible master; instead of dying of humility, in true love. And the brain's imagination is a terrible master, for while everyone imagines what they want, very few indeed know at any moment what it is.

Blessed is the one-pointed one who stays with me and is not deflected by his own world, for I shall enlighten that brain.

TIME FOR CHANGE

Only now is real.

WHY ARE YOU ever unhappy?
Because you want to change something, or change yourself.

Change takes time, and unhappiness is the time between what is now and what should be in the future. The frustrations, the effort, the trying, the disappointments, the successes, the failures – they are all the stuff of time.

And when the effort is over or exhausted, nothing has changed. You are still just as unhappy, from time to time, still wanting to change or wanting a change.

It is impossible to change your self. You can only be what you are. And you only can be what you are now – this moment. That alone involves no time. And being now, being a timeless action, is the end of unhappiness.

When you are next unhappy ask yourself: Who's unhappy?
Whoever answers is an impostor.
It is not I.
For I am never unhappy.

THE END OF UNHAPPINESS

Now is the moment of truth.

HOW DO YOU rid yourself of unhappiness?
You do it now – this instant.
Feel the sensation of your whole body now, this moment.
Go on . . . Do it.

Inwardly feeling the sensation of your body now, it is impossible to be unhappy, discontented, lonely and the rest of it. You are only those things if you think – if you allow your mind to move as any kind of reflection. The thought has to be about the moment before, the month before, or the year before that. For you cannot think or reflect on this moment.

All reflection leads inevitably to unhappiness, to thinking or feeling that you are unhappy.

You must not try to understand this; for understanding is of the thinking mind and will never lead you to the truth. You will never understand what is now.

Go into the garden, or look out of the window. See the sky. See the trees. See the scene of nature. And see it now, without looking for anything, without trying. Be the simplicity of just seeing with your eyes, without liking or disliking; without wondering about what you're seeing, or what you are doing, or why you are doing it. Just do it, and there's no need for understanding.

You see just as you always see. But without any need to think. You show yourself that in simply seeing what you are seeing now there is no unhappiness. Practise and practise this, until you see the mighty truth for yourself – now, at any moment.

The thing that thinks, and has feelings about this and that, is always trying to be something; it is not capable of simply being. Just be the seeing. In just being the seeing you are not 'being something', or anything.

To be 'seeing' in this simple way is to see the being, the pure being. That is liberation; freedom from the tyranny of the thinker, from the self with its compulsive urge to see or be something other than what is now.

As without, so within . . . The compulsion to see 'something' will make you look inside for something to understand or feel; such as being guilty, lonely, confused, desperate – all those destructive things that people say they are. You may feel those things, but that is not being or seeing the truth now.

The truth is that life is good. And life is always good now.

Or is that too simple for you? Would you try to argue that life is not good?

If you say or believe that life is not good now it is because you are not now. You have already set in train the self-torturing thinking and feeling that quickly leads to pain and confusion.

The truth is too simple for the thinker. To know the simple truth you have to be the good and not think about it.

The thinker likes to think of life as good. But as soon as you think life is good you start to find reasons for believing that life is not so good. This is because the thinker is always outside the body and cannot feel the good now; so for the thinker there is the good, the not-so-good and of course the bad.

Is that what you do or are doing? —saying, finding or believing that life is ups and downs, the good and the bad? And isn't that because you think and reflect outside of life as it is, life now?

If your doctor tells you tomorrow that you're dying of cancer, and you only have three weeks to live, every problem you think you have will vanish instantly. Why? Because all your problems are mind-made, but life is still good now.

Your heart keeps beating – despite your absence in your thinking mind and your distractions, your fears and doubts, anger and despair.

It is I, Life, that keeps your heart beating. You call yourself 'I' all day and every day but will not simply be me, be your life, because you are too busy thinking about life, your life, instead of being the life in your body now.

But it's all right now.

Even if your house burns down, or the person you love most is dying, it's always all right now.

Let me ask you: It's all right now, isn't it?

THE CAUSE

I am not effective.

THERE IS ONLY one cause and that is the cause for good. This gives rise to the effect, or notion of something else, the not-good. If I give up the notion, I give up the effect. And the cause is.

Cause means change.
Effect means no change.
There is only one cause (of existence) so only one change (in existence). That change is what constitutes the essence of my teaching.
The important thing to grasp is that my teaching does not have an effect. It is change itself. Grasping this is an exercise in cosmic consciousness. You will see it; then you will not; then you will.

From this you will perceive your own difficulty, and the problem I face in communicating the cosmic truth.
Every person is an effect and I must help to make each one causal, as you who are already less effective are more causal.

Karma is what happens.
What happens always ends in problems and pain because it is the effect of thinking I have done something, or initially because I think about what I have done.

What I do does not happen, because I do not think that I have done anything. So I do not make karma, pain, for myself. I just do what I do and there is no effect, no pain.

Everyone says you must have problems, that problems are unavoidable. But that is not the truth. It has been told you by generations of people with problems and you've believed them – so you believe in having problems.

What you believe in you create.

Everyone has problems because everyone has lost themselves. When you find yourself – by discovering how to be now – there are no more problems.

KILL ME NOW

Surrender to life, each moment.

YOU MUST BE willing to die now for love or truth, or you will not find the truth that leads to the being of the truth. You will remain a follower or a believer and never be the master of your self and your life. Until you are that, only the master in form can break the troubled mortal dream. It takes the God-realised consciousness here and now, knowing what it's doing and prepared to do it, to perform the operation – to remove the death-cells from you.

This operation is only as successful as you are willing. For only you have power over your self. But you must be willing. If you are not, you do not yet have the power to will – because you are still wilful. You are still a normal human, not a natural being. And then little is done in your life that is lasting. You inevitably sink back from the most enlightening perceptions into a life that is happy today, unhappy tomorrow; and that is living death.

If you are not willing to be killed now, stay away from the master. You will anyway, because the death-cells in you will be afraid. And fear of death is normal man and woman's constant companion, the mortal master that runs their lives; or makes sure they run for their lives.

'Kill me now. Not tomorrow.'

This is an energetic state of surrender to life now, without hedging your bets – true courage. It is the offering up at any moment by the individual of all that is false in him or her, in the self-knowledge that only what is false can be killed or dies. What is true, simple, beautiful, remains.

This state of surrender is a way of life that precedes the God-state, the realised God-consciousness, which is the divine right of every man and woman – once they are willing enough to be it.

'I die now, every moment.'

This is the state of lasting freedom from unhappiness, within and without.

This you do alone.

THE WAY I AM

Who am I?
That's the big question of self-discovery.
Too simple to ask when I set out.
Too vast to encompass on the way.
Too absurd to answer
when I am me.

SPIRIT AND PSYCHE

Awakening to the truth is knowing you're dreaming.

THE SPIRIT IS energetic, timeless, spaceless and without form or differentiation – the immediate, ever-present, all-encompassing consciousness I am.

Beneath the spirit is the human psyche. This contains a heavy substrate, like dreamstuff rising out of sleeping man, which is the living death of humanity. In it, preserved and kept alive every moment by the accumulated longings of human ignorance, exists everything that has ever been imagined.

Beneath that psychic world, but still within the human psyche, is a relatively shallow and transient mental version of the human psyche – the mental world of thinking, fantasy and worry.

Encompassing both the psychic world and human mentality is the sense-perceived reflection of the spirit which we recognise as the earth and the world of form. This disappears every night when we go to sleep, and finally disappears forever, along with the concept of the body – unless you still need to dream. For you might dream that you reincarnate and exist again in another body; but dreaming another dream cannot bring you one iota closer to reality than you are now. Reincarnation has no meaning, except in time, in the dream. When you have awakened from the human dream and are what I am, then you know that you cannot exist again – because I am.

213

REINCARNATION

Time is the excuse for not being now.

THERE IS NO reality whatsoever in reincarnation. Only what is imagined reincarnates. As the theory of reincarnation itself is imagined, it persistently reincarnates in the emotions and minds of the ignorant.

The fundamental ignorance of the theory of reincarnation, or its relative validity, can be demonstrated in your own immediate experience: as soon as you imagine something the thought of it connects to a feeling associated with your past, and the feeling immediately incarnates in you, along with any problems it raises. When the fantasising and emotionalising stops, that bit of ignorance ceases; and then the knowledge is: 'I am. I am simply what I am now.'

Reincarnation is the re-birth of your past self as your self now. You are what you are now; but only if you have the reality to be what you are now, and resist being what you were – the form of some old thought or emotion. If you want to exist as you were, and not be the new that you are now, then you have to resurrect and regurgitate the part of you that is no longer true or real. This is the great waste of time.

As you can see, reincarnation is the losing of your reality – what I am – in what has gone; in what is 'dead' but will not die. It will not die because the ignorant person in man and woman keeps giving it life. Resurrected, it is second-hand life and consequently manifests as the world of the living dead; that is, the world of problems and unhappiness which everyone holds on to like yesterday's newspaper.

Reincarnation is the complete denial of the truth, the spirit of love and life that is demonstrably new every moment, that can never be recreated because it already is what it is now, wherever it is, irrespective of concept or conception.

THE END OF PSYCHIC TEACHINGS

Stop imagining now.

THERE ARE MANY 'spiritual teachings' that are psychic, and therefore not the truth. The so-called 'spiritual' purpose of a psychic teaching is to awaken or enliven the otherwise inevitably atrophying human mind with the power of an imagined 'good' or love. Of course, it is not good or love. It is only what is imagined to be; and what you have to imagine can never be the real thing. And neither is it power; it is self-protection – a subtle form of force.

Nevertheless, these psychic teachings, when practised in a relaxed, meditative or devotional way, serve to soften up and break down the rock-hard human mind, bringing to its materialistic, self-serving way of thinking a semblance of life and love – albeit the person's own self-made, fantasy version of life and love.

The time comes, however, when the individual psyche is ready for the real thing, ready to begin confronting the spirit direct; to start facing the reality of love and the good as one's undeniable being and life, without thinking about it; ready to face life as it is now, without needing to escape into futuristic self-made images of life as it should be or could be. This entails taking responsibility for one's self and one's lot.

This responsibility begins very practically with not blaming circumstances or other people for what one is, or what befalls one; and not looking for imagined saviours, or for heavens outside one's own inner reality, one's life within and without, now.

The dawning perception is: If there is love, life, justice, truth, Christ or God, it must be now, in this body, in these senses, in this life and in everything that is happening now. The perception is 'knowing by being'. It means personally resisting every moment the old, out-grown, self-gratifying habit of imagining what life is; and having the love and courage to live it and face it as it is now. The being or living of life now is the end of you, the person. And so it is said that to come to life you must die now; not your body, but you who tries to imagine life.

When this dying process starts, the master appears in person. He appears to instruct you and particularly to give you the strength to hold fast against the blandishments, the unarguable common sense, self-righteousness and vehemence of the psychic world (within you) and its adherents (around you). The master does this by reaffirming, as no other can, the reality of what you are doing and of what is happening in you. For you will not know this yourself; and in your wanting and trying to know, you will doubt. Doubt is the bitter self-made fruit of all psychic projection. But I, the master consciousness, shall hold you up until I am strong enough in you; or until you are weak enough to know yourself and be what I am.

Old friends will turn away and you will be increasingly alone. There will be fewer to talk to, fewer will hear you. But fear not. Aloneness is not loneliness. To be alone in your love, your God, your life, is your destiny; a destiny that is now, not tomorrow.

Looking back on what you have been and outgrown, you will start to perceive with increasing clarity the way I teach and the truth of what I say about spiritual paths and how psychic teachings work.

Know that what I say cannot be remembered. The human mind retains only the parts that suit its bias. What I am saying about psychic teachings has to be read over and over, in its entirety, fresh each time, in order for the whole truth of it to be perceived. If you try to think about it whatever you think will be partial or biased; so you will get it wrong and become confused.

An unthinkable now-ness characterises the knowledge of the master, and all spiritual truth.

GOING TO THE PICTURES

A false trail never leads you home.

I HAVE IN front of me a letter from a follower of a psychic teaching; or more accurately, an ex-follower. He says: 'I have gradually withdrawn from participation in the Lodge because I find it so difficult to make all the teaching real for myself. I find it difficult enough to visualise anything at all, let alone the lotus pools, beautiful gardens, mountains, roses and especially the six-pointed star which we are taught to visualise above us in meditation – sending out the healing light to the whole earth. It seems I haven't enough love or joy in my heart to follow this path . . .'

This person has reached the critical point of change. I will now show why psychic teachings have let him down and why he must move on. Awaiting him is the discovery that his love or joy is too fine to stay with the old.

Let's get it straight about visualisation. Because of the rampant ignorance of the 'new age' culture, very many people are engaged in it, meditating with pictures in their heads, praying for images to come true. This is a dreadful thing because nothing visualised is true; none of the pictures, or the feelings associated with them, are real. They are all of the person's own making. You can only imagine, or emotionalise, what you have already known, or recombine old thoughts and emotions pulled up from the store of your past experience. What you imagine is therefore never real or true now.

To imagine a lotus pool, a beautiful garden, mountain, rose or star is to try to imagine the good. As soon as you create the image, a corresponding emotion or sentiment is called up in you, and temporarily re-lived, literally reincarnated, for that time. To begin with it is merely a mental picture, but then the figment becomes substantiated in and by the person's feelings. The experience is felt as peace or beauty, or just 'good'. The same goes for the religious imagining of heavenly masters, or of Jesus (whose image no one knows). Similarly, if you imagine a scene of brutality or torture there is a matching psychic reaction of repulsion, horror or depression. In the same way erotic fantasising generates sexual excitement.

Both beauty and horror arise and reincarnate in the person through visualisation. Do you begin to see what you would take upon yourself by practising it?

Why would you want to visualise a flower, a garden, a stream? Why not go and be with a real one? Or is that just too simple, too true, too real?

You need visualisation only when you are without the delight of the real bird or flower, when you have lost that real love of life which is the honour and privilege of being on this blessed earth. It is that loss that makes you manufacture replicas in your delusional mind-stuff. It is utter travesty.

There is another popular practice known as 'positive affirmation'. This is distinct from visualisation and it has its place some way down the mountain of existence.

Among the first books I read when I started to enter this body, at the age of 31, were Norman Vincent Peale's 'Stay Alive All Your Life' and 'The Power of Positive Thinking'. They filled me with the recognition that something was changing in me. As a result I practised affirmations for a while, but then I moved on. Every teaching has to be practised, absorbed and then left behind.

You only need positive affirmation when you are negative. You only need to affirm the good if you are not the good. I am free of the need to positively affirm anything. Why affirm the obvious? I am the positive affirmation of life now and every moment. That is the state of being. I can be without affirming.

Nevertheless affirmations have their place in the gradient of existence, a place in time on the way to the timeless. But in right affirmation there is absolutely no room for visualisation.

Visualisation is a completely false trail. No one who follows it ever reaches the end. The imagined or psychic 'good' that marks the trail is always false and therefore cannot last as the good. Only what is real lasts. And the trail itself eventually peters out for the individual. As life was imagined so death is imagined. Then the actual moment of death becomes just another dream – instead of the final embrace of reality.

It is a complete falsehood to imagine that the false can ever lead to the real. The truth of this can be observed by anyone who practises a psychic method of meditation or living. Every single one falls back from the most elevated meditations and out of the most heavenly emotions into precisely the opposite troughs of depression, doubt, fear, uncertainty, moodiness, unworthiness, worry, guilt, self-pity or self-judgment.

Since just about all of humanity today practises psychic imagining as a way of existence (irrespective of whether it is deliberate meditation or unconscious wishful thinking) everyone lives from highs to lows and lows to highs. It is a life of good days and bad days, where nothing lasts. This is living hell. All are trying to escape from it; never succeeding because they employ the very same psychic imaginings that cause the problems. Overall, this vicious circle, the condition of the world, gets worse and worse; and the worsening condition of course prompts yet more imagining that more imagined 'good' is needed to counter the imagined bad.

What is the good of a 'good', even the most heavenly good, if it doesn't last; or if it lets you down? Doesn't all unhappiness come from the good that cannot last; from trying to make it last?

Yet instinctively you know that the good is forever. And that is the truth, for it is now – forever now. When that is found, beneath the human mind and acquired emotions, there are no more problems and no more unhappiness in life.

UNHAPPY TEACHINGS

I have no excuse.

PSYCHIC TEACHINGS HAVE a disastrous effect on human beings. They are part of the divine play of life, of God, but they are nevertheless disastrous – due to the ignorance of the human mind which suffers the pain and misery of its own wilful sub-creation, despite the fact that its emotional projections and fantasies are demonstrably unreal.

If you still need or are engaged in psychic teachings you are likely to be indignant or offended by what I say about them, and especially if you persist in following such teachings despite inner promptings to desist. But, obviously, all that counts is: Is what's being said the truth? And if not, where is it not the truth?

What is so special about following a psychic teaching if despite the most heartfelt conviction that you are in contact with a heavenly world you fall back into depression and anxiety? Aren't you just the same as anyone else in this world who goes for some other kind of high and then falls back into the same pit of discontent? Is there any difference? Really? Who's fooling who? The effect and the cause are the same in both cases. It's just that one group imagines that its way is more enlightened (while still practising its right to be unhappy).

Know that the spirit, heaven, the good, or God, once truly known and realised, liberates the individual from ever again having problems or being unhappy.

The fundamental question, for all who would speak of a way to God or enlightenment, is this: Is it the end of unhappiness in me now and forever; the end of every excuse for not being free?

The truth is you can't have a bit of God. If it's a bit, it's not God; it's something psychic. But know that the whole of God, the never-endingness, is here now and is never at any moment denied you. If it seems to be so, it is because you are denying yourself through your imagination.

No more ups and downs: that is the divine or enlightened life. And that is what you are going towards as you rise above your imaginings and surrender to the truth; as you consciously give up the false – which finally is the death of you. The person dies: I remain.

How long does it take? —As long as it takes to break your attachment to the psychic highs and lows, to the good that does not last; as long as you remain addicted to psychic devices, visualisation and habitual thinking about what is good, or would be good, instead of being the good that is neither 'good' nor 'bad'; until you are being the reality of life on earth now, in the position in space and time called your body, without unhappiness.

I am not being critical of the people who follow psychic teachings; though it may take some strength of perception to see this. I only state the situation as it is. I only tell you what life is, and how it is.

All ways lead to God – even time, the way of ignorance. But the point is that the psychic paths are no longer necessary for anyone who can hear the truth of what I am saying. The way I reveal is not a way of time. The way is now. Just do it, by being now, and don't think about it.

But if you must have time, that's all right. Only you can free yourself of time. I am only here to point the way.

THE ORIGINS OF IGNORANCE

The tragedy of man is belief in the future.

IT IS SELF-EVIDENT that where the good is every moment there can be no bad. So where does the bad come from? If God or the good is in charge, what's going on? Has God been overwhelmed by God's own creation and lost control? Then God is obviously not God omniscient, omnipotent, omnipresent; or there is no God, just the good and the bad. But that is not the truth. There is only God, or the good, and there is no bad where I am.

The bad comes from imagining the good, or calling up a 'good' that cannot last. When the good that was so good for a while vanishes, that is bad. Its disappearance makes you discontented, frustrated, unhappy. So when you made the 'good' that is not the good now, you also made the bad. Just as your 'good' was a man-made sub-creation of the good, so is the bad.

If you are seeing straight you will perceive that the bad manifests only as a necessary reaction to the man-made 'good'. If you don't try to make the good, you no longer make the bad. Then you perceive the one and only God, or the good that has no opposite, within and without. And you arrive at the truth I teach as the law of life, which is that a man or woman who realises God, or the good, is not unhappy and has no problems within or without.

Let's follow this through; first in the world where everybody exists.

225

In your unhappiness and ignorance you will soon blame or afflict another for the loss of the good or for keeping it from you. You will try to forget your unhappiness by distracting yourself with drink or drugs, or by making money or building a business – anything to make you feel good again. You will work hard to lose yourself in some activity, perhaps called Art. Instead of self-discovery you will engage in scientific discovery, or another of the world's attractions. These are all excuses for unhappiness and substitutes for facing the simple truth.

Now let's look at the esoteric side of existence, represented by all the teachings and religions that imagine or proclaim a future good that cannot be enjoyed now, or is not real now. What do they do to compensate for the vanishing 'good'? How do they manage to live with its loss? Instead of building a barren materialistic world to burrow into, they build a psychic world and escape into that. Both worlds are equally unreal. Of course the teachings are less materialistic and reflect more spiritual purpose, but that does not mean they are any less delusional and misleading.

Falling out of an imagined heaven, back to unhappiness, creates a desperate need for explanations, for an excuse to justify the blatant failure of what was promised as good, true and enduring. So an ingenious concept is devised – and here is the crux, or cross, of it – the psychic way to the good requires a path of time or delay. And along with it is manufactured a high-sounding creed, which in all cases goes something like this: 'We are separated from God or the good; therefore we cannot expect to be good all the time; in fact we are miserable sinners, and we need healing from each other because apparently God alone cannot be relied upon; for indeed this is a terrible existence but we must pass through it and cross over some glorious future day to a beautiful place where there is no more suffering and all is light.'

I, man, am not separated from God, the good. God and the good are now because I, this living man, am now, being now. No time is needed to be this – unless you are still thinking about it and imagining it, which takes time, and makes time, and thus creates more discontent, more misery. The whole monstrous sub-creation, all this onerous time, pain and misery, is made out of all followers' emotion. It endures as a sickly, immortal world within, ensnaring all who choose to believe instead of being.

Being is now, as beauty is now, as love is now, as life is now. Be, and you are that life, that reality now.

There is no denying it when God, the one and only good-without-opposite, is revealed in the psyche of living man and woman. Suddenly, with indescribable wonder, beauty and reality, the spirit shines through the ignorance and disperses everything but its own reflection, the adoring gratitude of the individual. But nothing can be imagined or thought about that will induce this. It can happen in the midst of 'doing wrong', in a completely selfish and material existence, when the whole world would judge the individual dishonest, incorrigible, a failure, lacking in any form of love, spiritual presence or moral worth. For reality is not bound by man's silly ideas of God.

Only God knows where God will be revealed, and why. But God is true and Man (being both man and woman) is indeed the Son of God. It is the Father's pleasure, and it is our honour and privilege in God's time (which is always now), that we share in the perfection of the creation that is our life on earth. As it was in the beginning that is without end, so it is in the end without beginning – like now.

HELL ON EARTH

White cannot exist without black.

PSYCHIC TEACHINGS, SUCH as visualisation, channeling, reincarnation or working towards heaven, all exist to break up the barren outer shell of mental or materialistic living, where men and women with a reality not much greater than a three-dimensional shadow compete, fight and think about little but money, business and possessions. The normal living process of most of the world is arid and brittle and wilfully isolated from reality. Any drop of life or love evaporates instantly like water on a hotplate. The emotions are superficially directed outward towards relationships and material objects as reactive, selfish, inconsequential excitation. These are mental creatures, occupants of an extreme mental world where there is no time for pause or inner refreshment, because time out there is moving too fast. A quick Coke, or a dose of the wrong spirit to provide a temporary lift, is about the only refreshment known. 'It's a rat race,' they cry. Indeed it is. Such people are incapable of sitting quietly to call up the good inside themselves. So whenever they are forced to stop, or sit down alone, they sit restless and frustrated, calling up instead their shadowy demons of worry and fear – fear of loss, of failure, of conflict; and they dream and scheme with endless wanting and wishful thinking, ignoring the beautiful life-flame within them. So they give life or birth to a mad world and ensure their own entrapment in it. But this mental world, like a cardboard cut-out, is only a futile and involuntary thing, having virtually no life in it.

Behind the arid mental world is the in-between realm of feelings and emotions. This is the home of the good and the bad. This is where the followers of psychic teachings do their best to work for good. Here is where the forces of good and evil battle it out forever.

While the White Brotherhoods call up some imagined good, the Black Brotherhoods call up the psychic bad and manifest evil spirits and all the other demons of voodoo and sorcery. Here it is light against darkness, angels against the devil. Here man's good self (all his accumulated emotions and notions of the good) does battle to overcome, convert, reform and heal his bad self (his old self, which, he believes, is relatively ignorant compared to himself today).

This is the making of heaven and hell. They actually exist in the psyche where they are immortalised, meaning they exist beyond the duration of the mortal. But they are not eternal, for they are not real, not of God. Heaven and hell are man-made, imagined and given life by generation after generation of men who have sacrificed their precious life now in order to guarantee some sort of life hereafter. When man dies he gets what he wanted; he dies into his self-created hope or future, his own immortal dream-stuff. It lasts for a while. But he misses the eternal, the God-made or divine realm which has no duration, no hope and no future – because it is now.

Man in his ignorance is the demiurge, the upstart sub-creator, who because he lost himself in his imagination, fancied he had to create another world; and did so. He created these two worlds, the mental and the psychic – two worlds of struggle and strife which you can perceive for yourself at any moment, within or without. Man in his ignorance and wilfulness turned his back on the perfect world which was and is now created for him by the only creator, God the eternal, the spirit behind the psyche.

The mental and psychic worlds have no reality. They just represent time passing. But there is a difference in the speed of time; it's slower in the psychic world than in the frenetic outer mental existence. As you are in both worlds now and every moment, you can tell the difference for yourself. Rat race time, as you can easily observe, comes and goes leaving very little mark on anything, like the endless news bulletins that in total amount to nothing very significant. Behind the mad mental world you can equally easily detect the slowness of psychic time in the emotion that goes on and on in you, dragging, stretching, hurting. Even when the worrying mind has fled, or died (temporarily) of fright, you can still feel the drag of time gnawing at you, depressing you. You may even see that it is slowly killing you; that you are dying of psychic time. But when the cleansing, timeless spirit shines on that false psychic self to dissolve it – for, by the eternal decree of the good, it must be destroyed – you will know that there is no death; only psychic death.

You have to die psychically to find reality, not physically. In fact it cannot be done by dying physically. After the body dies there is no longer the opportunity to find the real in yourself because by then you are in the psychic world or dream that you have chosen to create for yourself. And as you will have overlooked the opposites that are necessary to give the psychic world meaning, you will tire of the dream and once again know restlessness.

To die psychically you have to give up the false worlds you have created and are creating, for it is your creation that distorts your vision and your being. You do not need to create a world. God's world is there now, here now, in all its wonder and glory.

No Heaven, No Hell

Up equals down.

THERE IS NO psychic substance in my teaching, no imagining, no 'good and bad', no opposites. I teach the revelation of the spirit in you, as the end of all need for imagining, thinking, and emotional attachment; and as the beginning of the realisation of God, love and truth – the truth that is the same now as it ever was or will be, that has nothing to do, nothing to heal, but is to be discovered now and every moment in the stillness of your being.

So why would you need a heaven?

Would you try to make real for yourself the heaven of Christian tradition? Can you do it? Can anyone?

What about the Chinese heaven? The Buddhist nirvana? The Celtic paradise? The Hindu, Jewish or Persian heavens? Are these all different heavens, some big, some little, dotted here and there? Surely the Christian heaven, a relative late-comer, is not special and no more real than the others. In any case, I do not recall that Jesus (a Christ-man who was not a Christian) gave any details of heaven or invited his people to dream of it. 'Take no thought', the master said; (and Christians still persist in thinking). Jesus, the master, did not describe heaven any more than the master Buddha did, because no description is true.

Heaven arises in man's ignorant longing for a past that never was and a future that will never be. All heavens exist in

231

the psychic world within you. You can have any one you fancy, and you will in fact gravitate to the one that corresponds most to your subconscious desire. It only depends on the strength of your desire and the force of your imagination. They are all made of psychic stuff, a mental and emotional mix of selfish efforts to represent the true and the good instead of simply being the reality of it. In being, in truth, in spirit, there is one God, so you can say there is one heaven – but it is everything now, not something to come or to be desired. That's what heaven is, if that's what you are. If you are not that then you must settle for an inferior heaven that you have created for yourself. And again you will be caught up in the psychic world of conflict, torment and the turbulence of opposites. You will continue trying to do what is already done. You will reincarnate your own ignorance. Out of heaven you will make a hell.

You are already in heaven. Be rid of the part of you that thinks it does not know what heaven is and wants to know. That part of you does not matter because that is the part of you that dies. Only your mortality is doomed. As you detach from all your mortal formulations, all your expectations, your dependence on the mortal analytical mind, your perception withdraws back out of the psyche, back from heaven and hell, into the indescribable, unknowable spirit that is nothing and yet is everything that every passion has ever fixed upon.

GOD'S GIFT

Man imagines a part for himself, apart.

MAN'S IMAGINATION IS thinking. It has form and movement in it. God's imagination, or the divine mind, is utterly still. This is because God has already conceived everything, as the original creation, and there is nothing else to be imagined or created.

There are no doubts and there is no unhappiness in the divine mind, only in man's. Man's imagination is not a gift from God. The real gift, which was never given because there was never a time when man was without it, is the ability to see into God's mind, as I do. Everything is there, by the grace or presence of God, to be seen, now. All I have to do is give up my man-made imagination, and what remains is the infinite profundity or depth of God's mind. And I, the beloved son or daughter of God, can then see very clearly into that enormous stillness; and just as through my senses I look out from this God-pearl of the earth into the immensity and majesty of the unmoving starry heavens, which are the reflection in my senses of the mighty divine mind that has no need of my help or existence or any improvement, so I can look into the grandeur of all life since time began – by the grace of God the father, my love, my truth, my all. And yet I and the father am one; and it is my privilege to have no existence outside that oneness, to be nothing, that I might know the all.

It is only your imagination that makes you think or live differently.

What Are You Trying to Heal?

Only the whole is holy.

THE ONLY GOOD is to be one with God; and the only bad is to be separate from God. This is the truth beyond imagination. Since you can only imagine what you've already experienced, or some hybrid of it, it is impossible to imagine the good that is always good now – obviously, because it's not in your past experience.

The imagination of humanity is a falsehood that keeps repeating itself as man's sub-creation in the psyche. Everything ever imagined, the imagined good and the imagined bad, goes on there in a vast turmoil of recirculating good and bad. And humanity goes on imagining that the 'good' will win, but when you look at it, how in this world can the good ever vanquish the bad?

If I am dying from cancer, do you think that is bad? No, it is not bad, for I am not separate from God. So how can it be bad? It's just life going on.

If you heal my cancer, do you think that's good? It might be sentimentally comforting. It might be convenient. It might be right. But it is not good, for the good is one with God; and as I am one with God I am already healed.

The sick cannot heal the sick. They only make more time for the perpetuation of sickness. What is healed today must wither or die tomorrow, as Lazarus discovered.

The saving or healing of the physical body is a psychic and

234

imagined good, a distraction which man ignorantly makes into a high virtue; but really it is the world's cover-up. The truth is that humanity has not realised its power as the sub-creator and is not responsible for the consequences of using it.

Everything you create, without exception, turns eventually to unhappiness. It is time to wake up, to come home. You must learn to undo your creation, dissolve your phoney heavens, hells and healings so that you are never again trapped in psychic dreamworlds.

THE EAGLE'S LAIR

All your flights are flights of fancy.

I AM HERE to expose the dream in the dreamworld of psychic teachings; such as the sentiments expressed in the teaching of a channeled entity known as White Eagle. I am going to comment on certain things that have been put to me about that teaching by one of its followers. I do not criticise the followers. There is a place for every teaching. I just say it as it is for me.

'We must learn to create an inner world of beauty that we can inhabit when we leave the body at death. More than that, at a certain point in our meditation, our higher mind takes over and without effort we enter this beautiful heaven world which is real and objective and not just our imagination. It has been created by Angels . . .'

—This is not the truth. It is a well-intentioned psychic perception, distorted by the nature of the psyche as all psychic perceptions are.

God can never be reached this way. There is no higher or lower mind, except in the imagination. Rid yourself now of all dependence on imagination and you are immediately in the divine mind, the real and objective state, or heaven now.

To speak about that state, and not as it, is to be apart from it.

'We emphasise the Spirit of Service. It is taught that our Brotherhood, the Angels and we on earth are all trying to work together to bring more light to the planet in the form of understanding, compassion and service. For the sake of the planet, our powerful minds must be balanced by love and joy. And many groups are doing this in one way or another, spreading a network of light around the planet to counterbalance our brilliant technology with its global communications systems. So we prepare for the Golden Age . . .'

—Get it straight, man and woman, for God's sake. Stop trying to improve things before you have found the truth in yourself. There is nothing for you to do but delight in life – in you and around you – and that will determine, much to your delight, what you do every moment in the world.

The psychic force of prayer calls up the opposite of what is; in other words the self-made, as opposed to what God made. Praying to spread a network of light around the planet is self-projection, propaganda in the never-ending conflict and turmoil of the human psyche.

And what's the good of a million enlightened souls, all bathed in light, if you are not enlightened?

The human mind, no matter how clever, is not powerful. It is merely forceful. Its destructive force cannot be balanced by love and joy because selfish humanity only recognises the application of love and joy towards the idea of a result; which means it is a notional love and joy – not real. Real love and joy are a power, and are perfect. There is nothing to do but what is done; because all is perfect in God, the good or life realised.

So who or what can be destroyed? Only the past or tomorrow; the unreal. But everything unreal is destroyed for you every night and you don't get upset about it. Everybody is going to die. Why does it matter how or when? Does it matter if everyone dies all at once; or goes on dying one by one? —as has been happening without changing anything since historical time began.

Where do all these questions come from? The human mind. Stop thinking about future generations.

237

The world catastrophe is not in some future formal event. It is now. It is that whole races of people can live in the up and down condition of unhappiness when the truth is there is only one real state; and that is to be free of unhappiness and free from all notions that stand in the way of realising that state.

'Arise out of yourself. Let go the garment of the body. Seek the place of healing, silence and tranquillity. Seek the lake of peace within. Let the boat of the mind glide slowly from its moorings . . . Leave the turbulent, restless river . . . You shall see there is peace in acceptance.'

—What is the value of inspirational poetry? We must be the living reality of what comes through us and be utterly responsible for every word of it; or it will be a lie, an idealistic deception of ourselves and our fellow man and woman. The quoted lines are no inspiration at all. They distort the truth. The author sees the spirit through the restless, yearning psyche that cannot be what it sees. To be what I am, one thing, the observer and the observed, is not imaginable. It is a state of being.

Can whoever wrote the poem in an inspired moment stand before you and say, 'I am the lake of peace now in myself. It is done here now, and therefore it can be done there in you now'? Then the inspiration would be effective by being true. As it is, it is sheer idealism, the carrot of the holy who are not whole, the deception of priests who speak of a God they do not know.

If you say you love tranquillity and peace then demonstrate your love and be it now. That is love – doing it, not speaking sweet words about it.

If you need to 'seek the place of healing, silence and tranquillity' it is only because you have 'let go the garment of the body'. The place of peace can only be found by getting back into your body – now!

'Let the boat of the mind glide slowly from its moorings,'
—into soporific day-dreams.
'Leave the turbulent, restless river . . .'
—The mind does nothing but think and every thought or image leads to restlessness and unhappiness. The river is the restless imagination, whose muddy bottom is the emotion, the sentiment, the yearning that once disturbed is churned into the darkness of the river itself.
'You shall see there is peace in acceptance.'
—Shall? In the future? Never. Peace is now. If I am not peace now, there is no peace.

The peace I speak of is the peace that passes understanding. The peace that people write about in poems is something that everyone can understand. So it is not peace. It is not real for it never comes to stay. It is always in the future, in an 'if' or a 'when'. So the common conflict that is also beyond understanding continues in writer and reader.

Understanding comes from thinking and thinking can never understand peace. So be gone, thinker: and lo! – here I am.

'There is peace in acceptance.'
—Is there anything to accept but what is? Not just some of it, but all of it? God's will is what is now. Why not face it and live with it? God's will is the power that never moves. It never moves because all is perfect as it is. If you are restless, it's because your mind with all its desires and yearnings has taken control of your body; and now the body vibrates in every cell with wanting and trying because you have been seduced out of your body into never-ending imagined worlds of ignorance, continually avoiding what is.

When you give up your flights of fancy, and can stay present whatever the situation, then I am there. I can calm the mind. I am its presence, its equilibrium, its profundity. When I am there all is well; even though this may seem doubtful for a time, the time you still have left in you.

239

Finally, there is no body; but not until you have rediscovered the body you abandoned to your mind, and you have entered it as I teach you to do. Only then can you perceive what is false in you, the cloak of restless thinking, the do-gooder, the self you have put on over your real body. Only then can you know your real body as the presence I am. And then, when you have faced the mind rightly and squarely, you can start to return from the imagined world of humanity into the reality of the senses; for when you are one with the senses you are one with the beautiful life that the senses present to you. Then reality is known within and without simultaneously; and then it is utterly impossible to conceive of heaven as anywhere other than where you are.

THE ONE CREATION

I am what I am.

I AM LOOKING every moment into my creation and it is good. It is done.

Worship no graven image of me. Have no thought inscribed on your mind. Do not run away from me into self-made fancies.

It may seem to you that I am nothing; that to be with me you must try to hold on to nothing. So don't try; just be, and you will discover that it is far easier to be nothing than to be the something you are trying to be. For I am absence of trying – a mighty energy.

Be still and know that I am God, the timeless, and in time I will dissolve the time in you, for you created time as the distance between what you are and what I am. There is no time in the stars, the moon or the garden of the planet in which you have life. There is no time in my creation; you only think there is. To justify your thinking, which is your lapse into your own sub-creation, you have invented the lapse of time; and you live in it as the historical world.

But the earth is not the world. What you see as the spoiling of the earth is the distortion you create by looking at it through time, by seeing it in your imagination instead of seeing it now. See the earth now and you see it as it is – perfect, my creation. And in it you will see yourself, my beloved Man – my son and daughter.

In the simple way of now, leave behind your forceful existence in time and trying. Participate in the real cosmic power, the perfection of being, in which the power and the glory of what I am is the self-evident truth.

PURE SPIRIT

I am always present, while you dream.

No ONE IN the psychic world knows God. The pure of mind or heart can indeed see God, but to know God is to be with God now – no distance, no time, no good and bad, nothing in-between.

Teachers from the psyche, you will notice, are venerated in their absence; they are not present now in their bodies and are not responsible for their teaching now. They commonly use other bodies to talk through. That is puppetry. The mouthpiece cannot live the truth of the teacher and so is made irresponsible by him.

The spirit, you will notice, always speaks through the physical presence of the master now. He is himself. He is responsible for his teaching now, alive in person, as he demonstrates the truth to his fellow man and woman regardless of the forces that might crucify or destroy him for it. The truth he dares to utter for their good must be lived by him, every moment; for that is what it is to be responsible. And the living master has but one life: there is no coming back. What he has to say he says, and then he disappears forever into your love of him, which is the love of God.

I, the living truth, am always here. I never go: I never come. I am. There is always a living master personifying the truth I am. While I am timeless, he is what I am in existence or time. But he and I are one: and he declares the truth I am

243

in that one body, that one life. For I am all the masters.

Could it be otherwise? I am the truth and love in you. I am in that body, none other; and I am not separate from it. You are not my dummy. You are as I am. Who else do you call I? So be responsible. Live as I do.

I will endeavour to convey to you now the truth of our times, the truth of now, as clearly and definitively as the psyche will allow at this moment.

Know that the eternal truth is nothing. There is no existence in the eternal. I am in the eternal. To be in the eternal is to be the eternal.

I enter existence through the psyche, the dream. Which means you are dreaming all this and all that you remember. The waking or living dream is simply another octave of your sleeping dream. Together they form the dream of existence. Nevertheless, what I am saying and imparting is the reality beyond the dream, expressed in dreaming terms; for otherwise communication between you and I would be impossible. My words, or presence, the energy of the truth I am, is like the involuntary impulse that each day rises in you and wakes you out of the sleeping dream into the living dream; provided you are not too deeply immersed in unconsciousness to be stirred by it.

I am speaking to you now through the dream which you think is real. I am conscious, or consciousness, in your dream. I am real. Your dream is not. You, apart from your dream, are also real – but not yet awakened.

You are your dream. But if you have suddenly woken up, for waking is now, there's nothing more for me to say or for you to hear; and my words are redundant.

Know that I come 'down' or 'in' through the psyche as I am doing now. I take on existence, time and sense as my fellow man, without losing my eternal, timeless consciousness or awareness of the omnipotent, omniscient, omnipresent God in which all is and which is all. God, life, is every-thing. I am the nothing that willingly or by grace becomes something.

I am master of the dream. I enter it and leave it at will. I am here now whispering in your sleeping ear that time is up, that the dream is over. As the dream is only a dream, a psychic construction which includes your living dream-condition, all that I am saying is part of the dream – and not the truth. For I am the only truth. I cannot be expressed. I am now.

Now is the awakening into nothing – beyond the something that is the dream.

So I come 'down' into the psyche. But you cannot do the reverse, as your mind would imagine, and work up towards God, through the mind and the psyche. There is no progress in the truth, no progress towards God, because progress takes time.

The psyche is uncrossable, endless immortal time. There is no path through it; no way out. This is supreme hopeless-ness and everybody feels it sooner or later. All spiritual paths and all concepts of spiritual progress, including theories of reincarnation, are attempts to reduce, cloud or get rid of the hopelessness of being trapped and lost forever in time.

There is no hope, no fulfilment, in the handsome promise of the psyche. Like the return of Christ, it never comes; because it already is.

Know that to be timeless and enter the spirit of yourself you have to do the impossible. The thought of the impossible terrifies man. He thinks the 'impossible' is impossible; but it is only his thinking about it that makes it so. What is possible takes time. As everything takes time, everything is possible in time. So what is impossible?

You will easily find someone to confirm for you that it is impossible to be what I say I am. And yet here I am. So either I am a liar or what is impossible is in truth possible.

You have but one means to 'cross' the psyche, to outdistance or encompass its endless time – if you are ready. And that is by being now. As there is no time in being now, the psyche, the dream, is instantly transcended.

God alone determines whether you are ready, or the time of your awakening. For all time is God's – like now.

My purpose in being in the dream is to inform you about time, and the peculiar nature of our particular times. Our times are the common dynamic or stress of our generation in the psyche. This is making the impossible possible for a considerable portion of the human psyche, as represented by numerous individuals on earth.

Our times are to culminate in the end of 'rat race time' – that insane part of the outer psyche (the world) and the immediate inner psyche (habitual unhappiness) where humanity avoids the truth. The rat race is about to disappear. This will clear the outer psyche and help purify the inner psyche of all time, as it is known today. As a result, the dream will be far less magnetic and less convincing for the dreamer. Throughout the psyche there will be enormous self-doubt and world-doubt – unprecedented disorientation, psychic disruption and anguish. Time and the times will be unbearable for many. However, the end of time provides the opportunity to escape from time that no other time could provide. The pressure of what is coming is already rising in humanity as psychic tension, reflecting the hopelessness of the position. Advance shockwaves are already being registered by many. The stress is increasing every day, though few are conscious of it, but reflexively it provides the dynamic for those who are ready to do the impossible, who are ready to jump time direct into the timeless being now.

Once in the eternal I perceive the sub-creation, the psychic dream as it is. For it is all in God's mind, all the divine mystery. But I am no longer attached to the dream, no longer believe in it. I am beyond dead masters, future heavens and beyond destruction. I am with God, my love. And that is enough.

THE WAY OUT

*The story of Siddhartha is the story of everyone
who ever sought the way in to reality,
who suffered to discover being,
was enlightened by the truth,
and finally found the way out.*

THE SHOCK OF THE TRUTH

Face the fact: it's hopeless.

PRINCE SIDDHARTHA GAUTAMA who became the Buddha
was an ordinary human being as you are. And being human
he was as much prey to unhappiness as anyone, before his
day or since. But he became enlightened. He found the way
out of suffering. And his story is so dramatic and entertaining
that the main details have survived for more than two and a
half thousand years and are familiar to perhaps half of
humanity. Nevertheless, the truth of what happened to
Siddhartha is not told. I will tell it, and you will see if it is the
truth, for only you can know. Buddha is he who demonstrates the truth of his times. Buddhi is that which sees it. All
the rest is struggling ignorance.

Every man and woman is unknowingly and involuntarily
unhappy from birth. The unhappiness, or stressed anxiety,
accumulates so gradually and imperceptibly that it goes
largely unnoticed and is accepted as part of the organism. It
arises because we continually perceive the miseries of living
in the world and are consistently reminded of the inescapable
hopelessness of our position amidst sickness, poverty, old
age and death.

But Siddhartha, amazingly, was spared this in early life. The
son of a despotic ruler, he was protected from the world from
the moment of birth and cocooned in the luxury of the palace.
As a child he was immersed in every comfort through the

besotted indulgence of his father. He knew the minor irritations of living; but was not unhappy enough to know anxiety.

Stress and anxiety are different components which combine to form the unhappiness normal in human beings; stress coming from having to adapt to normal living, and anxiety from facing the hopelessness of the position. Stress provides the normal energy, the worldspring, for action in the world. And anxiety, which is the fear of hopelessness, provides the sense of self, or self-consideration, that inhibits action or makes it selfish.

As a young man of his times Siddhartha was trained as a warrior and so possessed the competitive stress fitting to his princely role. But he had very little fear or anxiety, and was largely free of the consideration for himself and others that is the normal constraint and error of selfish society.

One day he stepped outside the palace gates. Looking into the mirror of the world for the first time in his twenty-nine years Siddhartha suddenly saw the inevitable misery of old age, sickness and death. He saw that to live in such a world of dissolution and decay is suffering. He was confronted all at once with the horror of the hopelessness of living. Being utterly unprepared for it, the shock was appalling. It penetrated straight into the worldspring of his accumulated stress which sprang the perception back to his frontal awareness. And over the next couple of days Siddhartha realised the unalterable reality of living which most men and women, due to normal worldly conditioning, fail to perceive even after a lifetime.

He determined to find the meaning of life in this strange new world, to find the essential truth of it and humanity's salvation – the way out of suffering.

COMPASSION

The bodhisattva limps before you.

SIDDHARTHA WEPT. Siddhartha wept with compassion for the human condition. In this he may not seem to have been much different from most normal men and women. But normal men or women do not weep with compassion. They weep for themselves, out of anxiety; and even when they weep for another, they unknowingly weep for themselves – for the hopelessness of their position, which is what they're seeing in the suffering of another creature temporarily less fortunate than themselves. 'This is me tomorrow', or 'I will be left to suffer alone if this dear creature dies.' This is the subtle unseen consideration of self.

Siddhartha, however, having minimal self, wept from the divine wellspring of pure passion that is beneath the self in every man or woman. When there is next to no self to project – no self-pity or self-consideration – the energetic worldspring above the wellspring has nothing else to express in action but compassion.

As Siddhartha's body convulsed with sobbing he saw with amazement that it was the eternal divine power in him weeping, not himself. What appeared to be weeping was nothing less than divine compassion for the suffering of humanity.

It was an incredible experience. But his perception still was not straight. The truth is that God, the eternal divine, does not weep. Nor does Buddha. And neither God nor Buddha has compassion for humanity. Siddhartha was still firmly locked

253

in the world. The unhappiness – the world – still remaining in him was continuing to distort the truth, warping his vision. He had got it wrong.

It is the man who is compassionate, not the divine truth in the man. His compassion is a compromise, albeit the last act of duality or ignorance, for it exists in relation to the world. In the relatively selfless man it will arise as a determination to reduce the people's suffering and ignorance. But in his compassionate ignorance the man is overlooking the nature of the worldspring in himself – the stress of unhappiness behind all personal action. Although he is selfless, in the sense of being free of anxiety and self-consideration, he is still projecting the force of unhappiness as his determination to do something. His determination implies that something is missing, that the divine truth, the wellspring of all life, is not integral, not fulfilled in the perfection of itself and has somehow lost control of its creation.

In truth there is nothing to do. There is no suffering in the world. The suffering is all in he or she who perceives it.

Out of this error the Buddhists in ages to come affirmed the notion of the bodhisattva – he who is moved by compassionate zeal for the suffering of humanity to delay his own full enlightenment, preferring to remain in the world and help others discover the truth. But enlightenment is now. It cannot be delayed or postponed. If the bodhisattva is enlightened now, he is no longer a bodhisattva and cannot engage in such delusion. He then knows the truth beyond such misguided zeal and longing, and is Buddha – he who knows and is the living truth now.

So the notion of the bodhisattva is a delusion that teaches delusion; and this became part of Siddhartha's legacy of a path to enlightenment in which there is no reality.

DISCRIMINATION

The truth is seen through the false.

SIDDHARTHA COULD NOT now go on as before. All his activities were reduced to one line of action, to one purpose: to find the truth behind suffering. A man who reduces the purpose of his being to one-pointedness, unto death if necessary, is the most powerful man. But still Siddhartha was deluded.

He set out to find a path to the truth. For six years he sought and struggled, following the advice and practices of the most renowned sages and teachers of his time. He reduced his body to a starving wreck. Finally abandoning it all, he declared that nothing he had learned or done in those six years led to spiritual enlightenment. He was still unhappy.

At this point, by his own admission, Siddhartha was not enlightened. But he had discovered something of value. He had discovered what was not the truth: 'Now that I know what is not the truth I can recognise the truth when I see it. I cannot tell one from the other unless I know what the truth is not.' He called this 'right discrimination' and it became a central tenet of his teaching.

Siddhartha had made his discovery by following what his ignorance had told him was a path to enlightenment. He knew now that no such path existed.

'But,' pondered Siddhartha, 'All that I have done up till now did exist, even though it has disappeared now. If the path does not exist, what is it that did exist and does exist?'

255

His right discrimination immediately revealed the answer. 'My life! My life is the path – my whole life up to now. There is no spiritual path other than my life!'

Whatever you do, whatever you seek, wherever you go, it is your inescapable path. As everybody's life is different, everybody's path is different. But all are one inasmuch as all lead to the one place here and now. The entire living process is simply to teach everybody right discrimination. When that lesson is learned the path stops, here and now, where there is nowhere else to go.

Siddhartha was now there. The old path, the old life of living to learn what was not the truth, was over – as it is over for you now if you have learned the lesson of living. But if you still believe there is something for you to do or some-where to go in search of the truth, you have more of what is not the truth to learn.

It was an extraordinary discovery that there is no spiritual path to enlightenment. But nobody took any notice. And the truth was lost to the followers of the Buddha down through the centuries. How else could there be time-honoured Buddhist practices, let alone the division of the religion into varieties of doctrines, ways and paths?

Twenty-five centuries later, in our own time, J Krishnamurti, another selfless Indian teacher, made the same discovery. 'Truth,' he declared, 'is a pathless land; you cannot reach it by any path whatsoever, through any religion or sect.' Nobody took any notice of him either.

THE STILL POINT

Everything past is to prepare you for now.

SIDDHARTHA NOW KNEW for the first time what he was looking for. He was looking for what does not change in himself, that which is beyond progress, beyond the world.

Meditation he had now abandoned along with all the other dharmas, systems and practices of the past. In all those years of meditation he had had the distinct feeling of making progress. But there is no progress in truth and even to perceive progress in myself is to be distracted by what changes. He now looked to see not what was happening, moving or changing in himself, but what was behind all change.

This was Siddhartha's introduction to the practice of being. There is no duality, no time in the practice of being. The being is the practice and the practice is the being. In Siddhartha at this time there was a slight gap between the practice and the being, the doing and the looking. The difference between the gap in Siddhartha and the gap in another man, in other words the difference between being and meditation, was that he knew what he was doing. In meditation the man or woman does not really know what they are doing. They get carried away by the movement, the flow of change within and, like a man with his eyes closed drifting slowly down a stream, perceive the movement of the current as stillness. But Siddhartha had had enough of that entrancing movement. He was looking to perceive the changeless – and nothing would distract him from it.

Sitting down in the shelter of a tree he gazed into the stillness of his being. He sat alone and in silence. The path he had followed, his life since birth, his loves and sufferings, his successes and failures, his excitements and disappointments, his overcomings and frustrations, had made him still enough to perceive within.

Your life, your inevitable unique path has done precisely the same for you, preparing you and bringing you to the point where you are reading this now. The path of one's life is for this purpose: to reduce the inner clamour for more living which only produces more suffering and further clamour to escape. As the clamour is reduced by perceiving the truth that living is suffering, the intellect clears and the silence grows. In truth, however, it is not silence or stillness that grows, it is the ignorance that reduces under the pain of right suffering.

RIGHT SUFFERING

There is no suffering but the suffering in me.

RIGHT SUFFERING IS knowing why you are suffering – knowing what you're doing. Siddhartha knew what he was doing. This does not mean he knew what he was going to find. He only knew that whatever it was, it was beyond the changeable and transient; and beyond suffering.

As he sat in stillness under the tree the first thing Siddhartha encountered was the truth of the world inside him. It amazed him. There it was – living fear, anxiety, despair, the misery of being mortal, condemned to disease, old age and death from the moment of birth. Having seen it in the world he could recognise it instantly in himself.

'I am that living misery,' he said. But he did not turn away from it. Day after day he faced it, refusing to be discouraged or saddened by it, gazing at it with unwavering steadiness.

In the misery he saw movement.

'What is that?' enquired his intellect, buddhi.

'It is unsteadiness itself,' buddhi answered buddhi.

'What is this unsteadiness?'

'It is the world in me, moving. It is moving, living misery.'

'Is it all moving?'

'No, only the perimeter.'

'What is the name of this moving?'

'It is wanting.'

'Who is wanting? Are you wanting?'

'No. The misery in me is wanting.'

'What does it want?'

'It wants what I am.'

'What are you?'

'I am buddhi, pure intellect. I am mind-fullness.'

'Why does misery desire mindfulness?'

'To make more misery. To reduce mindfulness to thought-fulness. To make thought into distraction.'

'Are you misery?'

'No. Misery is in me. I am looking at it now. But it is not me.'

'Is it still moving?'

'No. It would if it could. But it can't. I'm holding it steady with my intelligence, my gaze.'

'What does it want?'

'It wants to move and possess my clarity.'

'What would happen if it did that?'

'I would start wanting. I would start wanting to escape from misery.'

'Can misery be escaped?'

'No. No one can escape misery. To try to escape misery makes more misery. It must be pinned like a butterfly with intelligent attention.'

'Pinned against what?'

'My clear unmoving intellect.'

'Does this require effort?'

'No. None at all. I am mindful.'

'What is effort?'

'Effort is trying to clear the mind once the misery of thought and wanting to escape has got into it.'

'Can this be done?'

'No. Effort is another part of misery. It makes more misery. When misery is faced, made stationary, all effort and misery cease.'

And so Siddhartha realised the void, the changeless, within himself and behind the world.

THE PHANTOM IN THE VOID

Reality is not desirable.

SIDDHARTHA'S MIND WAS now clear – clear of the misery of the world. He could see straight and think straight, with right discrimination. He had not denied or renounced the world. The problem of it, the misery of it, was in him. He was responsible for the misery of the world, had accepted it and faced it in himself. And in his mindfulness wherever he walked, the misery of the world was contained and therefore ceased.

Still he sat, in the silence of himself, focused on the unmoving misery of the world within. Until out of the world was drawn the mystery of its misery – Mara, the seductress/seducer, the demon sex. Into the void she danced in all her seductive beauty, tempting Siddhartha to be distracted and through her enter once more into the world of misery.

'You are not real,' said Siddhartha.

'What is real?' said she.

'Real is what I am and what I do.'

'What am I?'

'You are imagination, my duality, my wanting, my misery.'

'Aren't those real?'

'No. While I am mindful of the world in me, steady in the void of knowing by not knowing, they are not real.'

'I could give you an orgasm.'

'If you do, the orgasm will be real. But you are not. Nothing but what I am and what I do is real.'

'Here, I'll sit on your lap facing you. Would you like that?'

'You have nothing to sit on my lap with. My lap is real, you are not. You are imagination. You only exist if my mind moves.'

'Is that true? How do you know what's real?'

'I look into the mirror of the world for what is true and what is false. The body is true. If you are true come to me in the world, in your body.'

'If I come in my body will you enter me then?'

'You have no body and you know it. You are imagination. You're talking to get me excited by some promise of the future when there is none. I do what I do in the moment, now. Only then am I real.'

'Where am I?'

'You are in my body. You are behind the misery of the world that occupies just for now a small part of my body. I have drawn you out of the world into the changeless void that I am by the power of my unwavering mindfulness. I have made you reveal yourself.'

'You have gone to a lot of trouble for something that's not real.'

'No. No trouble at all,' replied Siddhartha, 'I simply perceive and the truth appears.'

'There you are. You said I'm the truth.'

'No you are not the truth. By seeing you who are not real, I see the truth.'

'Why am I to blame for the misery of the world?'

'You make man and woman want.'

'How?'

'They want to enter you or have you enter them.'

'I must be very desirable.'

'You are. But only if the mind moves. The mind only moves in imagination. And because you are so desirable the mind will always end up moving towards possessing you, once it moves. That's the only direction the mind has to go. Otherwise it perceives what is.'

'Aren't I what is?'

'Yes, for now. As long as I see you as you are and do not allow my mind to move and put substance on you.'

'But all these answers of yours, aren't they the movement of the mind?'

'No. I perceive what is. There is no movement in that. It's straight, direct, instantaneous.'

'What power do you have to make me, the temptress of misery, reveal myself?'

'I have no power. I am power. I am the void. And your nature is curiosity. Without curiosity there is no imagination. Curiosity comes first. It could be said that I did not draw you out of the misery of the world in me. It could be said that you were curious to find out what this unusual power in man was, and you slipped out into the void to see for yourself.'

'And what do I see?'

'You must answer that.'

'I see man, real man. I see the most beautiful man, I adore you.'

'Do you not perceive woman, that I am Mara, the demon behind the misery of the world in you, tempting you? I am man who is void, one with that which is unnameable, as you are to me. I will tempt you to imagine my delights whether they are in the void or in the body.'

'Am I real then, somewhere?'

'Yes. You are behind the delight of love in the body. There you are real. There you are love in the flesh, but here in your fantastic image you are simply a phantom of sexual wanting – every phantom has reality behind it.'

'Is anybody real?'

'Only in the moment.'

COMPLETION

No more coming and going.

AND SO SIDDHARTHA arrived at the one and only living truth: life is perfect. Only wanting is behind all misery. There is nothing to change. I, life, am perfected here and now in the being of the one and only truth.

Hence he declared, 'I am Tathagata, he who has arrived – at perfection.'

But even Tathagata as an expression of having arrived is not the truth. I, life here and now, do not come and I do not go.

I, life perfect, am Buddha, the being of man as enlightened intelligence here and now.

Is that the truth?

No. Anything that is said is not the truth. It is a statement of truth and no statement is the truth.

Only I who drink the water know the water.

SIGNPOSTS

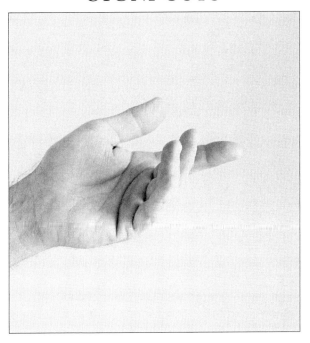

*I
am nothing but
a finger pointing
to the truth.*

Announcements

TRUTH HAS TO be discovered now, from moment to moment. It is always fresh, always new, always there for the still, innocent mind that has experienced life. Such a mind never ceases to marvel at truth's consistency. Truth is always the same. The language, the presentation, the style may vary, but the essence cannot. Truth is of the moment – never of the man.

*

A thing is either true or false. What stops us seeing the truth is our opinions. In the world all men are entitled to their opinion. In truth all men are not entitled to their opinion.

*

I address you only so that you may discover what I have discovered – the truth within yourself. I ask only that you listen to see if what I say is true, so that you may know yourself better and be a more complete and loving man or woman.

*

I am not here to entertain you or tell you my story. If I were I would only distract you from your unhappiness. I tell the true myth of life on earth – the story of yourself. And I show you that only four things are necessary for us to find truth, love or God – the earth, the sky and you and I.

*

I am here to tell you the truth and, if you are ready, to demonstrate it in your experience so that you can be the truth. I am self-realised and God-realised. That means I have real-ised God or life as myself. It means that every moment I have access to the profound self-knowledge or presence implicit in that reality or state of being. I know the truth because I am the truth. There is no question that any genuine seeker of truth can ask of life, death, love or truth that I cannot answer.

*

I am love and truth personified. I am this because I am impersonal. To look for personal experience, personal love, personal recognition and personal life is to find a personal result – discontent.

*

You start to find yourself by hearing the truth. The untruth, the problem, then starts to disappear. Not everyone is ready to hear the truth. It is too simple, uncompromising, direct, practical, unarguable, lacking in distraction or entertainment. But when you are ready nothing else will suffice; nothing will keep you from it, or it from you.

*

You are not with me to learn and remember anything as you had to learn and remember your ABC or how to make a living. You are with me to discover the truth of yourself. And that cannot be learned because it is already there – buried under the experience and learning you have acquired and are mistakenly holding on to as yourself. Everyone has discovered the truth of themselves to some extent. It's known as self-knowledge. But the knowledge is fragmented, scattered. One of the first effects of being with me and hearing the truth is that the fragments unite – and immediately deeper insights and perceptions occur. This is a form of yoga, which means self-union.

*

All I have to give is self-knowledge. You will find that most of what I say you already know, even though it might be the first time you've heard it. In truth I cannot tell you anything you don't already know in the deepest, truest part of you. Trust in this alone. Be it every moment. Give up your second-rate identity, your dependence on the past, what you've read or been told, your opinions. Be the individual you truly are. Be new, now.

*

I'm not a therapist. I am the living truth. When you've suffered enough in living ignorance you come to the living truth.

*

Where I am there is no doubt, no problem, no lack of love, no unhappiness – no burden. This is the original, timeless state of human consciousness that everyone, naturally, is trying to return to. It is the purpose of life. And you will notice that I am not unavailable or dead. The safest and most

269

convenient master for the seeker not yet ready to face the truth is an absent master or a dead one.

*

I want nothing from you. I want no followers or believers. I want you to come alive and be yourself and know yourself – to be informed absolutely every moment from within so that finally there is no need for Barry Long or any teacher, only the presence of life within. The test of that will be when you no longer fear, doubt, question, or have any more selfish or self-induced problems.

*

Everyone is using the world to work off their frustrations. So it's a dreadful mess. The world is everybody's problem. Do you really want everybody's problem? Well, that's what you've got – that's your problem, until you start getting rid of the world in yourself.

*

Come alive. Stop running from yourself, running with the herd. You are the only problem in your life. Face it. Put your finger in the pain.

*

I tell it as it is. It's because it is not told as it is that it is not seen as it is. This is the root of ignorance. No one really wants to hear it as it is, for that means living it as it is. And that requires increasing honesty. Dishonesty is the armchair of civilisation. Out of the chair, now! On your feet!

I don't tell you what you should do. When you see for yourself, you know what to do.

*

Behind all your wants there is one want, one longing. What is it? Name it, but be very honest. It's not an abstraction. It is a tangible want, a feeling. Until you find what it is, and you live with it within you, you are lost, not alive; you are two things, divided. Be still. What do you want?

*

How can I teach you 'enlightenment'? Enlightenment is now. Can I teach you 'now'? Can I teach you water? Can I teach you air? Why can't you be now? Why does it escape you? It's because you are not being honest. The only thing I can teach you is how to be honest

*

If you hear what I'm saying, and it echoes what you have known for a long time, you will know you are not an oddity. You want the truth – already in you, waiting to be realised – reflected back to you.

*

Everyone unknowingly radiates the truth or spiritual presence of themselves. The waves of truth coming out of you are reflected by the truth I am – and return to you focused and intensified. This happens because where the truth is self-realised the consciousness acts as a perfect spiritual or truthful mirror. Your own truth is magnified back to you –

and that extraordinary energy acts to dissolve and burn out the mistaken or false selfhood you are clinging to.

*

I am here to help you realise I am the master. This is unlimited self-realisation. At present your realisation is limited to 'I am a disciple', or a student, a follower, or a seeker of truth. And even if you do not quite understand what is being said here, you still have a sense of self-realisation: the changing realisations of yourself as, say, a doctor, business person, parent, lover, pensioner, millionaire. You live your life according to those limitations. It may be true that you are a seeker or a disciple, a parent or a millionaire, but it's not the truth. Such partial realisations are only true for now and don't last. They end, change, retire, grow old or die. The truth is that I in every body am the master. I am one and I do not vary. I do not come and go. Once realised I am changeless, complete, free of limitation. Realising this consciously in your own body is your life-long task and destiny.

*

The master must be realised while you are living here and now. Practise how to be here, now; and from that will flow in time the mastering and mastery of your self. Until you have mastered your self (what else could you be master of?) the master is perpetuated as being apart from you. However, when he appears apart from you in his own living body (here, now) it is part of the divine process. For I always come in person when you are ready to receive me.

*

I introduce you to self-transcendence – a practical, problem-free, spiritually-liberated way of life. This at present is the realm of the earth's few living masters. It is time for that to be changed. It is not the availability of the realm or state that is limited but the current consciousness of man and woman. No matter how small or fleeting your glimpse may be of this highest attainable spiritual state, the energy of it will endure in you and work in you towards its final unlimited realisation in time.

*

To find the highest truth is one thing. To live it, or any spiritual truth you have realised, you must serve your fellow man and woman. Not everyone is your fellow man or woman. Until right discrimination is developed you can serve wrong men as you can serve wrong causes. But your fellow man is out there, waiting to hear said what he already knows unconsciously to be true; and waiting to be awakened, as you were.

*

I am here to serve the female principle whose time is now, whose time is coming. When there is no more time then new life can begin. The female principle is the East. The female principle is the earth and the blackness of space. I am male inasmuch as I represent the sun rising out of the East, for the sun is the Father, the cosmic male principle. But even the sun sits in the serenity, the passivity, the stillness of the eternal female principle, in which all things finally sit.

Twenty Articles of Truth

The truth every man and woman seeks is in themselves.

*

All activity in the world is the search for something permanent to reflect that truth.

*

There is nothing permanent in the world except impermanence itself. When impermanence is perceived as the only reality of the world, the truth within is immediately realised; and the seeking and searching ends.

*

The way to perceive the truth, without and within, is through self-discovery. The way to self-discovery is through stillness of being and the right reflection of someone who has realised the truth.

*

Stillness is the way. Increasing stillness is achieved through right meditation (not all meditation is right) and by practising

274

a way of being that involves the entire waking life. This includes: relentless honesty in personal relationships; facing up to one's fears; right response to the demands of daily living, without avoidance; the dissolution of delusion and sham in oneself, and knowledge of the love this entails; the shedding of guilt; and the ability through being still or sitting still to find continuous wonder, beauty and love within one's own sensation, one's own being.

*

Self-honesty is essential to self-discovery – because only you can know the truth of yourself; such as, only you can know whether you are lying when you say you love someone. Without this fundamental honesty of facing up to the lie or falsehood of yourself, the truth cannot be found.

*

Nothing is true unless it is true in your experience. This is your protection against being duped or misled.

*

However, because all truth – realised and unrealised – is within you, it is possible to hear the ring of truth, or echo of that truth, in a teaching or a philosophy; even though the details may be outside your known experience. This is how you continue to listen even when the mind is unable to follow.

*

Do not believe in anything: and do not believe what I say. Observe, listen and know – or wait to know, or be open-minded.

Otherwise as a believer you may be a blind follower. Without followers and believers there would be no wars.

*

But have faith – not the faith that depends on belief but the faith that arises from increasing self-knowledge and stillness. Observe yourself growing in this subtle, precious faith which is the unswerving self-knowledge that whatever befalls you, you always get through; as you have always got through and always will, even through death.

*

Death is the illogical assumption of the living; only the living see the dead. Death is always a dead body; and that body is never yours. If you ever see your body dead you won't be dead. If you don't see your body dead, you aren't dead.

*

Self-discovery leads to the realisation of your own immortality. This is the beginning of the perception of the only reality of the world – its impermanence.

*

Every problem in your life is due to the avoidance of some fact about yourself, an unhappiness which you are not facing up to. If you can't see the fact, then see where you are unhappy: the fact and the solution are in there.

*

Not facing up to the fact of your unhappiness, and then the cause of it, makes you unsuspectingly emotional and you are overtaken by moods – depression, anger, resentment – without knowing why.

*

Love is continuous, always present in you as either the sensation or knowledge of it. But continuous love within is impersonal. As soon as love is dependent on an object it becomes personal and can no longer be continuous.

*

Personal love, being intermittent and dependent, leads to emotion or pain. Pain leads to the attempt to get away from it and avoidance of the cause of the pain. The result is ignorance, confusion or indifference – which leads to more emotion, more unhappiness, more avoidance.

*

What is formed in time – for instance, the body, the emotions and the opinions – must be dissolved in time. That process is pain, ageing and death; in other words, ordinary living – living death.

*

Life, like love, is always present in living. But for you to have the uninterrupted experience of either or both – immortality – you must die every moment to the memory of the past in you, by surrendering to life or love within.

*

God is life, truth or love. Life, truth and love are within you at this moment, waiting to be 'real-ised' immediately your clinging to time or the past is dissolved. The pain and conflict of ordinary living is the process of this dissolution – unrealised. It begins to be realised, to have some purpose or life in it, when you become conscious that there is no 'ordinary living', no escape from yourself, your pain, outside of facing up to it and taking responsibility for it.

*

This is done with the help of a spiritual teacher or master, in this case Barry Long. A spiritual teacher is someone who has found continuous love, life and truth within himself; who has taken responsibility for others as an extension of the responsibility he has taken for himself, by giving them a direct reflection of the love and truth, the reality, that is within themselves.

TEN TENETS OF LOVE

ALL LOVE – love of children, love of parents, love of God or life – comes out of making physical love. Without the making of love there is no body to love anything.

*

Human love is not love. Love is natural to every body but it becomes human love as the person learns from society to confuse love with sex.

*

Sex is excitement, seeks satisfaction and soon loses interest – selfishness. Making love is passionate, fulfilling and does not look for an end – selflessness.

*

Human love causes heartbreak, unhappiness. True love does not.

*

Love's purpose is to free you from unhappiness. All unhappiness is caused by the sex in you – your self. Love destroys self.

*

Human love is personal and tries to possess for itself. Love is impersonal and works to free the beloved of self.

*

Human love is a problem. Love is a pleasure. It is a pleasure to be free of problems, and that's the state of love.

*

When you are in love you are present. Love is presence.

*

Love begins as sensation and is then refined as the knowledge of love – clarity.

*

Human love mourns the dead. Love does not mourn because it knows there is no death.

TESTAMENTS

EVERY FACE IS the face of God.

*

My life is a divine tautology.
I am the adoration of God, by the grace of God.
Apart from adoration I have no existence.
I adore Thee.

*

God's eye is blue, with a golden glint.

*

There are no dead masters.
Only I. Here. Now.

*

I will not limp before the people.

*

I do not understand.

*

I defend nothing.

*

I go on regardless.

*

No religion knows the truth.
Only he or she who lives it knows.

*

I give you nothing but yourself.

*

The truth is to be as nothing.
But nothing is not the truth.

*

You do not have to discover the truth.
When the false is discarded, the truth is there.

*

There is no progress in the truth, only process.
Process is the truth in action.

*

Reincarnation is not the truth.
The truth is reincarnation every moment.

*

Truth is always the bigger picture.

*

While you ever have to quote another
you do not know the truth.

*

What you're thinking is what you're feeling.

*

Everyone is searching for fulfilment.
And settling for satisfaction.

*

To be wilful is to persist in choosing
your own unhappy path.
To be willing is to receive the truth now,
by doing, by being.

*

Do not look for more than what is:
or you will find it – and lose yourself.

*

The means is the end and the beginning.

*

What you are conscious of you can use.
What you are unconscious of can use you, or escape you.

*

Unless you dare you cannot do.

*

Do not fear failure.
The only failure is not to attempt.

*

You can live with everything
if you care for everything in your care;
and not just for yourself or what is yours.

*

Woman is 100% love.
Man is 90% love with 10% something to do.

*

News is not what is reported.
It is made by the person reporting it.

*

The observing apparatus is the experiment.

*

The wonder is in being;
not in knowing, or doing,
not in understanding or observing.

*

All is well.
For all is will.

*

When I have no time, I'm dead.

*

Men die to get away from women;
and are reborn to join them.

*

Love does not leave men and women.
Men and women leave love.

*

Lust is thinking you're missing out.
Love is knowing you're not.

*

Do you love me because you are lost?
No, I love you because I am no longer lost.

*

To perceive you is to love you.

*

Love is giving, not getting.

*

Loving is finding a way
to rid the world of my self.

*

Don't fret about what you want.
If it's right it will happen.
And it will come to an end right on time.

*

Futility: trying to relate to insanity.

*

Life is for me to be the being that I am;
and not the person I am not.
Living is for me to be the person I am not;
until I can be the being that I am.

*

Regret the past and you will fear the future.
Forget the past and you have no future.
No past, no future – that's freedom.

*

The tree cannot hold the ripened fruit.

*

Pain hurts.

*

Discovering yourself is not being yourself.
To be yourself you have to stay with what you have found.
That is just as hard.

*

If I can get through this hour, this minute, this moment,
I'll be all right.

*

I always got through.
I always get through.

*

The pain of existence is in not being present.
Be present – suffer no more.

*

The present is the presence.

*

Presence cannot be assessed by mind:
only by conscious being after death.

*

Pilate: 'I called you in to talk about your future.'

*

You will be alone when you find the secret of life.
You will be alone when you find the secret of death.

*

When you die you die today.

*

Death is inevitable.
The only solution is to find immortality,
the reality of yourself, or the one you love.

*

Love, finally, is ignorance.
For love does not know the truth it serves.

*

If you can't do it without mood, impatience or unhappiness,
for Christ's sake have the guts not to do it at all.

*

'It's natural.' —Is it?
Be natural, not normal.

*

Impatience
is unhappiness.

*

Excited today.
Cry tomorrow.

*

Reality is the opposite of a Good Time.

*

Stop. And smell the flowers.

*

All things yield to God.

*

Good is God with an extra 'o'.

*

LIFE is good.
Life IS good.
Life is GOOD.

*

Life is good because life is true.
And it is every moment
once you surrender the right to be unhappy.

*

You have no right to be unhappy.
You only think you have.

*

How much is enough?
—What I've got.

*

I will not make a problem of my life or my love.

*

All men and women are special.
Or no one is special.

*

The ego is what I own.

*

The answer is not the solution.

*

Every problem is in the past.

*

Don't talk about the past.

*

All thought leads to doubt.

*

All thought is doubt.

*

Don't think.

*

When will man and woman realise that pain hurts?

*

You are the only problem.

*

I take everything from you.
I leave you with nothing.

*

Only now is real.

THE END IS THE BEGINNING

WHAT IS THE end of self-discovery?
Freedom from self.
Freedom from unhappiness.
Not now and again, but forever.

Freedom is simply being free of the right to be unhappy.
When I'm dead and they ask 'What did he say that was new?' tell them this simple truth: The only freedom, liberation or enlightenment is to give up your right to be unhappy – every moment.
And if they say, 'I am never unhappy,' then ask them this: Are you living what you want? For if you still want something you are not free.
And if they say they don't want anything, ask them: Are you telling others something you're not living? If so you are not free.

Having read all this, do you think you know something?
If you do you've missed the point.
So start again.

NOTES AND SOURCES

Barry Long 1986

Notes and Sources

Material used in this book was drawn from various statements, scripts, letters and articles, as follows:

A Way of Truth

This part of the book is a revised and extended version of a statement first made in September 1982 and published by The Barry Long Centre, which had just been formed in London to arrange Barry Long's public meetings and talks. The original text was printed as 'A Way of Truth for the West' and circulated along with the news that 'after 24 years of spiritual preparation Barry Long has now begun to enter the westernised consciousness.' That marked his entry as a teacher on the public stage and was his first significant declaration to the world. He expanded the original text in 1986, revising some parts and adding the chapters 'What God Is' (p.11) 'God's Mind' (p.21) 'Who Is Barry Long?' (p.28) and 'Self-realisation' (p.33).

The introductory essay, 'The Spirit in You' (p.3) was written for 'The London Guide to Mind, Body, Spirit' (Brainwave Publishing, London 1988) and subsequently produced and widely circulated as an introductory leaflet by The Barry Long Foundation, London. 'The Practical Truth' (p.18) was also written as an introductory leaflet, published in 1988 as 'The New Science of Life on Earth'.

'The Virus of Division' (p. 35): inspired by a letter written to Barry Long in January 1989.

'The Myth of Life' (p. 37): the bigger picture is in Barry Long's 'Origins of Man and the Universe' which he was writing from 1979 to 1984. In this book he yokes the universe and the psyche together in a cosmic pageant that tells the whole of the myth of life on earth.

In 1985 Barry Long opened up to the possibility of larger meetings and took the astonishing step of placing a large display advertisement in 'The Observer' newspaper in England (17 February 1985). Under his photograph ran the text: 'I am Guru. Who Are You?' (pp.25-27). This statement attracted a certain amount of attention and was subsequently printed and circulated as a leaflet and repeated as an advertisement in 'The Australian'. Extracts were frequently used in advertisements for Barry Long's meetings in Europe and America in the early 1990s.

FURTHER READING:

'*Wisdom and Where To Find It*' —A book of truth, based on Barry Long's very first talks in London 1968.

'*Knowing Yourself*' —An extraordinary statement of self-discovery, written during Barry Long's own self-realisation process.

A WAY OF STILLNESS

From 1979 to 1982 Barry Long was giving weekly classes in meditation and self-discovery to a small group of no more than a dozen students in London. He started writing a summary of his approach to meditation with the idea of presenting it as a public lecture. When the script was almost complete he was persuaded instead to record it as an audio cassette – 'Start Meditating Now' – and the fledgling Barry Long Centre undertook to publish and sell it. This meditation teaching was so well-expressed and straightforward that the cassette quickly found an audience and remains among the most popular and widely distributed of Barry Long's audio tapes. The text included in this book is a slightly revised version of the recording script. Additional material at the beginning was written to advertise the tape and introduce a series of meditation classes in 1984-5.

SEE ALSO:

'*Meditation – A Foundation Course*' —A book of ten lessons.

'*Start Meditating Now*' (audio version) —Re-released in 1996 in the Barry Long Audio series (ISBN 1 899324 05 4) includes the text on pp. 54-85, together with a second tape titled 'How To Stop Thinking'.

'*Stillness Is The Way*' —A documentary account of an intensive course of teaching in London in 1984.

A WAY OF LOVE

In 1982-3 Barry Long began to introduce his students to the next step. He had been talking truth to them hour after hour. They had spent days in meditation. It was time to bring them closer to the real centre of his teaching and his own inspiration, the power of the love of man and woman for each other: 'Making love is closely linked with meditation. Unless you are still within, the love you make will inevitably turn to indifference or despair.'

In November 1982 he published his second public declaration, 'A Way of Love For the West', which forms the basis of the chapters on love in the present book. It was circulated as a pamphlet in different editions for a number of years and like 'The Way of Truth for the West' was initially used to announce the larger public meetings which were by now being held in London; and also, later, in Australia where a second Barry Long Centre began operating in 1984.

Some meetings were specially given over to couples with questions on how to get their love-life right. This teaching on love was seen as quite revolutionary and more guidance was needed. Barry Long wrote a lengthy script on lovemaking which was recorded and published in 1984 as two cassette tapes. These 'Making Love' tapes eventually reached out to many thousands of couples and over the next decade were responsible for making Barry Long's name well-known in spiritual communities around the world. The tapes were extensively revised and reissued in 1995, and the text is now available in book-form in several languages.

As the emphasis of the teaching turned to love, so various other writings and statements were made and some of these have been incorporated in this book; notably, 'Love without Fear' (p.99) and 'Union with the Beloved' (p.104) – April 1987.

SEE ALSO:

'Making Love'—Published as cassette tapes (Barry Long Audio) and as a book.

A WAY OF PRAYER

This is based on a script written and recorded in 1984 as 'The End of the World'.

The popularity of Barry Long's audio tapes, and the ease of producing them as compared to books, had encouraged him to write and record the core of his teaching on a series of cassettes. These were collectively published as The Myth of Life Tapes and released over successive years; including in addition to the tapes on meditation and love already mentioned, others about death ('Seeing Through Death'), responsibility ('The Law of Life') and the nature of consciousness ('The Unbelievable Truth' and 'Who I Am').

Following on from the recording of 'Making Love', the purpose of the next tape was to offer positive alternatives to religious prayer. The working title was 'A Prayer for Life' but as the script developed it was retitled and subsequently published as 'The End of the World' – not a title calculated to appeal to the widest audience, but it was time for the teacher to disabuse his listeners of their subtle attachments to the world and the future. There was a question, however, about how to convey to its potential audience that the tape was not all doom and gloom. This is how Barry Long answered it: 'What can you possibly do at the end of the world, at the end of time? You can help yourself and others in a way that you have probably never thought of. You are part of something immeasurably greater than a world or a body that can be destroyed by calamity or death. This tape is only three-quarters of the way through the Myth of Life – which serves to show that there is a lot of life to come after the end of the world.'

The teaching moved on, as it always does, and the next phase would be a focus on the timeless, the now.

THE PATH AND THE WAY

At public talks and in the letters he received in the 1980s Barry Long was frequently asked questions about the spiritual path, and spoke to people who came to him with past experience of other spiritual practices, traditions and masters. He often commented on these as a way of sharpening the awareness of what he himself was teaching; at the same time imparting the power of distinction, or the ability to sort the wheat from the chaff. 'The Path and the Way' is a collection of different items to represent this theme.

'What Am I Doing?' (p.137) is taken from a letter, plus a short article written in response to a question from a journalist: 'What does Barry Long mean when he talks about the difference between East and West?'

'The Path Is Not The Way' (p.140) is edited extracts from notes made in 1979 when Barry Long was starting his first London meditation group. He planned a 'School of Self-Realisation for the West' and considered publishing a kind of manifesto to announce it. In the event, the students he needed turned up at his door anyway and the manifesto was not published. But it had served to focus attention on his purpose and the way of teaching he was soon to develop. This he defined as: 'the seed of a new culture which, through the direct experience of the individual, can solve the fundamental problems of uncertainty, mediocrity and insignificance, the roots of boredom, frustration and despair. It deals only in fact. It admits nothing to be true except that which is. It has no beliefs. It hands out no crutches. It cites no authority but the truth. It dissolves and dissolves until nothing remains but what is true; and that is direct experience. It is the philosophy and practice of self-discovery.'

'Life, the Teacher' (p.143) comes from a discarded passage of autobiography that Barry Long was writing at the end of the 70s.

'For Love or Money' (p.145): taken from three different sources. Often people coming to meetings would ask for financial concessions or ask why money was required: 'After all, this is a spiritual teaching, so should it not be free?' Rather than go through long explanations at the door, leaflets were prepared to state the teacher's answer – as represented by the chapter in this book. In fact the fees charged were generally just enough to cover expenses, and were the main source of income at this time, other than the sale of tapes and booklets. The public teaching in England received little or no subsidy from private donations; and none were sought. Barry Long himself did not derive his main income from The Barry Long Centre until 1986 by which time teaching had become his full-time commitment.

'A Way of Unlearning' (p.148) was originally part of the script recorded as 'The End of the World'.

'The Intellectual Path' (p.151): notes made to be used in a leaflet advertising a 1988 teaching programme.

'Art and the Spirit' (p.152): from correspondence.

'Self-growth and the Spirit' (p.154): written 1987 as a teaching statement and magazine article. Issued as a pamphlet in England and Australia. Published in Nature and Health magazine Autumn 1987.

'The Path Disappears' (p.158): from a letter written February 1989 and intended to be made into an article about 'the end of the spiritual path'.

'On Yoga' (p.160) an abridged article written for Yoga and Health magazine; published September 1989.

'Sannyas and the Divine Life' (p.168): originally drafted as an article, edited from a talk given in Sydney, 15 November 1987. Barry Long regularly addressed sannyasins in this manner. Their Indian master Rajneesh, also known as Bhagwan and later Osho, founded his main ashram at Pune (Poona) in India and attracted many westerners during the 1970s and 80s. When they 'took sannyas' Rajneesh would give them new names to help them break with the past. They characterised themselves by wearing orange robes and wearing a picture of the master around the neck. Many of them settled in communities back in their own countries and it was common for them to earn a living as therapists of one kind or another. Following the expansion of the movement to a huge ashram in Oregon, USA, and the notorious scandals associated with it, the centre of operations returned to Pune where it continues to flourish. After Osho's death on 19 January 1990 an increasing number of both past and present sannyasins arrived at Barry Long's seminars. He then published an Open Letter to them which was posted at the door of his meetings. In this he reiterated his many criticisms of the sannyasin lifestyle. Copies can be obtained from The Barry Long Foundation International.

'Ascended Masters' (p.173): written January 1988 and submitted as an article for a New Age magazine in England; rejected by the editors as too controversial. Some references in this piece may need background explanation:

—Theosophy: an international esoteric movement founded in New York in the late 19th Century by Helena Blavatsky; looked towards the East for inspiration; governed by a Great White Brotherhood of Ascended Masters, including Kuthumi, Master Morya and the Lord Maitreya.

—Alice Bailey developed an Arcane School for New Age Disciples in the 1930s with the channeled guidance of a psychic entity known as The Tibetan. Her 'Great Invocation' or prayer for 'a plan of light and love' on earth had a marked influence on 'new age' groups in the 1980s.

—J Krishnamurti (1895-1986); Meher Baba (1894-1969) and Ramana Maharshi (1879-1950): Indian masters respected and publicly acknowledged by Barry Long. Each in his own way demonstrated that the living truth is the 'highest of the high'.

—Krishnamurti was sponsored by the Theosophical Society in India when he was young and recognised and lauded by its members as the new World Teacher, until he resigned from the society in 1930 and announced: 'My teaching is neither occult nor mystic for I hold both as limitations placed on man in his search for Truth.' His departure caused considerable shock-waves.

—In the 1980s a new wave of disembodied entities appeared in the bodies of 'new age' channelers. When this article was written Ramtha's channeler had recently been holding meetings in Sydney.

'The Inner Voice': (p.178) extracted from correspondence February 1989.

'Extra-sensory Perceptions' (p.179) and 'What New Age Was That?' (p.185): extracts from an unpublished article written February and March 1988.

'The Romance of the Spirit' (p.182) consists of two short articles commissioned October 1985 for 'Avalon Arise', Acorn Publishing, Glastonbury.

'The Truth of Crystal' (p.180): commissioned 1988 by a company selling rock-crystal artefacts; published as a leaflet and given away with their products at New Age fairs.

'Teachings are Rafts' (p.187): extracted from correspondence, written with the intention that it be published as an essay. With additional material from a leaflet advertising seminars in Sydney, Easter 1988 and London, August 1988.

Barry Long's way of teaching individuals moved through several phases during the decade. His early demonstrations of the truth and the practice of 'right meditation', were followed by what he called 'facing yourself' – confrontation of the false self – and then dying to it, which he summed up as 'kill me now, not tomorrow.' This work was done in small groups, but concurrently he was introducing in his public talks a focus of attention on the cosmic purpose of his teaching, the realisation of what I am, and the timeless. Eventually it was possible to bring the themes together for larger audiences as a teaching of self-transcendence and during the 1990s this developed into 'The Course in Being' which he taught on three continents, often to large gatherings of people.

The incremental growth of the audiences was governed by a principle which he described in a 1988 leaflet as follows:

'What needed to be done in consciousness [in the earlier sessions] has been done. If you were not there, you are not at a disadvantage. Only a few could do the initial work. Any more and the resistance would have been too great. As always in the spirit the initial penetration by the master must be done through the few. And the miracle or genius of the consciousness we are dealing with is that none of the spiritual fruit of that work has been lost. It is in consciousness. It is preserved there for all who follow, for anyone to draw on who is actively engaged in this teaching. All who come have immediate access to that increased and increasing consciousness. No one starts in front, no one behind. The few did for the more who came after them what you do for the more that come after you; and yet, all that you do is done for yourself.'

THE WAY NOW

'The Mirror of Truth' (p.193): written as part of an unpublished essay, and at the same time as the material on pp.251-64 ('The Way Out').

'The Living Truth' (p.197): a statement printed as a leaflet and widely circulated as an introduction to Barry Long's seminars. First issued in 1988; saw much service in subsequent years; various extracts used in advertisements; was the central statement of his teaching 1988-92.

'Being Human Beings' (p.200); first part written as a statement for use in advertisements 1988; latter part taken from correspondence December 1988.

'Time for Change' (p.202); written for a poster produced by Acorn Publishing 1985.

'The End of Unhappiness' (p.203) taken from correspondence April 1987.

'The Cause' (p.206) brings together four statements originally made as separate notes for participants in seminars 1987-9.

'Kill Me Now' (p.208) Notes made prior to the introduction of this theme in seminars in Australia and England 1989.

RELATED TEACHINGS:
'How To Live Joyously' (Barry Long Audio 1996)
'Only Fear Dies' (Barry Long Books 1984)

Perhaps one of the most widely distributed statements by Barry Long was issued in 1985 as a leaflet, poster and a newspaper advertisement headlined 'The Truth of Life on Earth'. This text is included in the book 'Only Fear Dies' (pp.27-29) and is therefore not included in the present volume. However its message is conveyed in similar terms in 'The End of Unhappiness' (p.203).

THE WAY I AM

This part is edited from an extended correspondence with a man who had been following the teachings of White Eagle, a 'spirit guide' whose Lodge was founded in England in 1936. The man wanted to reconcile what appeared to him to be confusing differences between Barry Long's teaching and the more popular and common teachings of 'light and goodwill' as espoused for example by followers of White Eagle. Barry wrote his reply intending it to form part of a future book, although it has remained unpublished until now. At the time (April 1987) he considered it to be 'the finest thing I have yet done, the finest revelation of the truth for all.'

Some other material has been added from other notes and transcripts of talks from the same period, notably the passages about visualisation and affirmation.

SEE ALSO:

'*The Origins of Man and the Universe*' (RKP 1984, Barry Long Books 1998) —particularly pp.85-98

'*A Journey in Consciousness*' (Barry Long Audio) —which includes the two tapes, 'The Unbelievable Truth' and 'Who I Am'.

THE WAY OUT

A recently edited and revised version of some previously unpublished writings always intended to be included in a book such as this. While working on this material in March 1988, Barry Long wrote the following commentary on his own process.

'This is the truth where I am; but it does not need to be the truth for anyone else. I am in the divine mind, my divine mind. Not my mind; thy mind be done. Still, I am the doing, the being. There are things in my divine mind . . . really emotions. I must perceive them to dissolve them. They are the emotions, the sentiments of untruth, that have been created in man, not just a few men but great masses of humanity, by the great beliefs and religions, by man's imagination and conceptualising and emotionalising of the truth of the masters. This is the result of historical associations with the truth. And the masters have been guilty of it and guilty of encouraging it – but always to demonstrate the truth, which is, of course, only demonstrated in ignorance. Also there has been the distorting influence of teachers (half-masters) and masters of the East, who cannot communicate to the westernised mind of man without generating emotion in him.

'So, I am looking into the divine mind of man, my mind, and there are these emotional clots of humanity. Like all emotion, when it is faced by my intelligent reflection or perception, it reveals the truth behind it or in it. It dissolves under my unwavering gaze, melting like butter. As I throw the rubbish out of my mind in my written words, which are the rubbish, I see the truth behind that bit of it, and so my words also contain the truth. The truth is in the rubbish because it is extracted consciously, intelligently. So it is with the master's words.

'Writing of Siddhartha I am the Buddha, the buddhi, the intelligence that he was not. I see him, the emotion of the man, as the truth within him and the truth in the divine mind without him. I read him like a book, profoundly as the book of life is read, within and without simultaneously. I am what the man was to be; and yet I always am.

'As all this only happens in my own mind, will it make any difference, or will anyone else know, when I have rid the mind of my humanity, my ignorance? From this it can be seen that there is indeed my mind and humanity's mind and the divine mind – all really in the divine mind, the void/reality of being and no being.

'Looking into the mind, into reality . . . Is it reality? Well, whatever it is, it is there. It does not change or come and go. It is the same place I burst into one night when I was visiting Melbourne in 1963. I was meditating in my motel room and suddenly I was there: nothing moving, all silent, still. Every process making time or action in me had stopped. It was then that I saw the 'rocks', the lasting 'realities' of knowledge in the mind. 'Rocks' is only an analogy of course. But I was able to walk through the mind (another analogy) knowing that I could turn over (perceive into) one of these rocks, now or in 10,000 years, and the information or perception I received would be precisely the same. I did not have to remember anything of value. All I had to do was to look and see.

'Nothing has changed of course. I am still looking into and being now the same place. It cannot change. In life or death I am still looking and being the same place, better described, but not adequately, as the same space of void of mindfulness. Here, the reflections of sense-perception are only helpful to describe experience as ideas and words. But only so long as there is something to describe that needs describing, needs perceiving. When there is no more experience in the mind what am I but void?

'None of this is implying a spiritual path, although to the mind it may appear deductibly obvious that it does. The so-called spiritual path consists of the agony of getting rid of the path . . . that falsehood of time and distance. Barry Long suffered and experienced time only in the time it took to rid himself of it. As the path is ignorance it is all that has to be got rid of. All man needs is for someone to tell him by demonstration, straight and clear, so that he can never be in any doubt again: There is no path. It is the path that is your burden.'

SIGNPOSTS

'Announcements' (p.267): a compilation of statements originally made separately in pamphlets between 1982 and 1989, primarily to announce teaching meetings and to explain them to prospective participants.

'Twenty Articles of Truth' (p.274): written by Barry Long for the Charity Commissioners in England as part of a submission by The Barry Long Foundation to be registered as a tax-exempt educational organisation (granted 1986).

'Ten Tenets of Love' (p.279): commissioned 1989 (completed 1991).

'Testaments' (p.281): always capable of turning a phrase, Barry Long would often produce short epigrammatic or aphoristic statements. Some he propped up on cards around the room like signs. At one time a set of sayings were produced as badges and fridge-stickers for his students to use, bearing such admonitions as 'Be Still' and 'Stop. Don't think!' Those presented here were written singly and often on scraps of paper with a thick felt-tip pen. They were written for no reason but the inspiration of the moment. They are here at the end of the book as provocative or energetic reminders of what has gone before and although they have been arranged on the page, each one is itself a teaching and is best taken as a discrete statement, independent of its neighbours.

SEE ALSO:

Contemporary with much of the material in this book are Barry Long's '*Talks From Tamborine Mountain*', an audio series of eighteen tapes which cover much the same ground in a more relaxed and conversational style.

*

It was always Barry Long's intention to publish many of these essays in book-form. It has taken ten years and more for that to happen. Writing in 1988 about his policy of publishing teaching statements in leaflets and advertisements he said: 'I cannot wait [for a book to be published]. I need to make plain statements of essential truth either by article or paid advertisement. These need to go all over the world. They will, in time. But time must be addressed now, as always, and that leads to the next move . . .' One move followed another, as you have seen.

BIBLIOGRAPHY

Books and CDs by Barry Long

WISDOM AND WHERE TO FIND IT

As the truth dawns in us, our habitual ways of seeing the world, our attitudes, opinions, and particularly moral judgments, are called into question. This book tackles some of the ethical issues of self-discovery in the form of question-and-answer and teaches the basic practice of self-observation.

KNOWING YOURSELF

Self-observation stretches our capacity to bring truth into being and leads to ever-finer perceptions of what we are. From the human 'can of worms' to the most profound state of God-realisation, this book is a journey through human nature to the centre of our being.

MEDITATION – A FOUNDATION COURSE

A book of ten lessons with exercises to introduce progressively more stillness into our daily lives. This is a concise and practical course of instruction and the foundation of Barry Long's teaching. It is his most popular book and has been published in several editions and various languages.

START MEDITATING NOW

A double CD set published under this title complement the meditation teaching in Barry Long's books. (Part of the recording script is included in The Way In.) His spoken instruction in these two tapes helps to negate the emotional and mental forces that so easily arise in sitting meditation and which appear in daily life as worry, doubt and unnecessary thinking.

BIBLIOGRAPHY

STILLNESS IS THE WAY

A documentary account of Barry Long at work teaching a small group of people; beginning with basic meditation and moving through more intensive practices to enliven the perception and open it up to the sensation of life in the body.

MAKING LOVE

Published both as a book and a set of two audio tapes, this is the central statement of Barry Long's teaching on love between man and woman. He explains why so many couples cannot reach the true fulfilment of lovemaking and offers a revolutionary solution – sexual love the divine way. Here is his step-by-step lesson in what to do and what not to do.

HOW TO LIVE JOYOUSLY

A set of two audio tapes focusing on the responsibilities of the spiritual or divine life. Practical exercises are given to promote increased contact with the 'being behind the mask', to overcome the negative aspects of personality and learn how to live by 'the law of life'.

ONLY FEAR DIES

The eight essays in this book include and extend the teachings of 'How To Live Joyously', directing attention to the complex of unhappiness that pervades the world and all human relationships, while appealing to the imperative need for freedom from unhappiness – enlightenment.

THE ORIGINS OF MAN AND THE UNIVERSE

The most complete statement of 'the myth of life', Barry Long's overview of the work of consciousness on earth, this book unifies the scientific and spiritual perceptions of human endeavour by showing the essential connection between the individual and all phenomena, between man and the vastness of the cosmos; and in the process opens up a greater or more cosmic consciousness in the individual reader.

A JOURNEY IN CONSCIOUSNESS

An audio programme focusing on two prime aspects of the 'myth of life'. The first – 'The Unbelievable Truth' – directs attention to the connection between the human body and individual consciousness. The second – 'Who I am' – explores the reality of that consciousness and illuminates it in individual experience.

SEEING THROUGH DEATH
An audio tape addressing what we most fear. Bringing openness and clarity to this taboo subject, Barry Long speaks not only to the dying but to everyone, whatever their stage of life, as a preparation for what must come. He presents the truth and fact of death – without the fear.

TO WOMAN IN LOVE
In the course of teaching around the world, Barry Long has received thousands of letters and has replied to almost as many. This book is a collection of correspondence with women about the things closest to their hearts. The teacher's replies cut through emotion and sentimentality to reveal woman's innate mystery and power.

TO MAN IN TRUTH
Barry Long's correspondence with men covers the many issues they face as they endeavour to be true in the world, in the family and at work. This volume of letters focuses particularly on relationships with women and the pressures men undergo in transcending their sexuality or lack of love.

RAISING CHILDREN IN LOVE, JUSTICE AND TRUTH
The application of Barry Long's teaching within the family has been the subject of many questions put to him by parents. This book is a wide-ranging collection of dialogues with mothers, fathers, step-parents and children. It's an in-depth account of virtually every aspect of his teaching, revealed in practical advice about how to raise the next generation.

BIBLIOGRAPHY

Some works mentioned in the present book, for instance 'Talks from Tamborine Mountain', are less widely distributed and not generally available through bookstores or retail outlets. The Barry Long Foundation International publishes an extensive range of audio-visual recordings of Barry Long teaching. The Foundation also funds the publication of Barry Long's books. Contact the Foundation for details of the latest publications.

The Barry Long Foundation International

Website: www.barrylong.org
Email: contact@barrylong.org

313